GREAT GRIMSBY

A History of the Commercial Port

Written & Compiled by
Garry Crossland MA and Captain Chris Turner
with the assistance of
Associated British Ports

Published by T&C Publishing.

Copyright © G.J. Crossland & C.E. Turner 2002.

ISBN 0 9543051 0 8

Designed and printed in England by ABP PrintSolutions, Hull

Acknowledgments

The authors would like to express their appreciation to the following individuals and organisations for the assistance that has been willingly provided in compiling this publication:-

Colleagues and staff of Associated British Ports; David Cowell; Brian Clarke and Cosalt Limited; DFDS; Michael Fish, Archivist of the Great Central Society; Bernard Greenberg; Peter Moore, Linda Roberts and the Grimsby Evening Telegraph; Dave Hewins; David Hopcroft; Bernard Huntley; The Illustrated London News; Fiona Service and staff, North East Lincolnshire Council Grimsby Central Library; Andrew Tullock and staff, North East Lincolnshire Council Welholme Galleries; Frank Priest; Steve Pulfrey; James Sutcliffe; Michael G. R. Stamford; Tom Walkley; Norman Wilsea.

In addition a special expression of gratitude is conveyed to Mandy Jervis, Brian Lingard and Colin Broadley for their advice during the proof reading of this manuscript.

Dedication

This book is dedicated to the many men and women who
have, over the years, played their part in the
various activities associated with the
day-to-day operation and development of the
Commercial Port at Great Grimsby

*The profits arising from the sale of this publication are to be divided
between the Cleethorpes Inshore Rescue Service
(Registered Charity Number 1085020)
and the Child Development Centre Appeal,
Diana, Princess of Wales Hospital, Grimsby
which forms part of the North Lincolnshire and Goole Hospitals
NHS Trust Charitable Fund
(Registered Charity Number 1054935)*

Contents

An aerial view of the Royal Dock looking towards Cleethorpe Road. The two entrance locks can clearly be seen either side of the Dock Tower with the jetties used for loading coal from Yorkshire and the Midlands dominating the background. Both of these structures were removed during the 1920's/early 1930's and a new concrete jetty provided at a cost of £53,233 in 1932. (Chris Turner)

Foreword

The coincidence of anniversaries in 2001, celebrating 800 years of Great Grimsby's Charter and 200 years of commercial port operations, was the spark to create this chronicle of Grimsby's port development.

In all things, history impacts on the future and this is certainly true when considering the way in which ports have progressed over the years. An example of this is illustrated by the strong influence experienced by traditional ports following the imposition of labour registration and control in 1947. The National Dock Labour Scheme was regarded as a necessary response to the uncaring nature of early port employers. However, its implication over the next 50 years was to directly result in the decline of many well known ports. The changes, considered necessary during the middle of the Century, were adversely effecting port infrastructure and therefore required modification. Reforms implemented in 1989 are now helping to shape the present port industry and build upon the strong foundations developed in the past.

Location is the other defining factor affecting the commercial success of ports. Those surrounded by large populations were initially prevalent. However transport developed, not only to match, but often became the catalyst for industrial growth. Ships got bigger and ports needed deeper water. Ports in the UK have to accommodate a large tidal range and it is desirable for vessels to remain afloat. This resulted in the construction of docks enclosed by lock gates. Tides still dominate the daily routine of ports, as can be demonstrated by the twice daily procession of vessels making their way up the Humber with the oncoming high water.

Grimsby, with its extension at Immingham, has coped well with these factors and flourished. However, if asked about the Port of Grimsby most people, including local inhabitants, would say "that's fish, isn't it?". The commercial success is not so widely known, although this year, 2002, sees the 150th anniversary of the opening of the Royal Dock. Years of progress resulted in national recognition in 2000, when the Port of Grimsby & Immingham achieved the title of UK's busiest port, handling 10% of the nation's seaborne trade.

Dennis Dunn OBE
Director, ABP

1

Introduction

Grimsby has, for almost 150 years, been synonymous with the Fishing Industry. The arrival of the first migrant fishermen and their families in the mid-1800's formed the foundation upon which the 'World's Premier Fishing Port' was created. Its renowned reputation for the handling of this single commodity tended to overshadow its long established commercial activities. The post of Dock Master at the Fish Docks was even regarded to be of a greater seniority than the same position at the Royal Dock. It has only been in more recent years that the contribution of the Commercial Docks, towards the sustained development of the Port, has been recognised.

The Old Dock, later to become the South Arm of Alexandra Dock, was constructed over 50 years prior to the opening of the first Fish Dock. It provided a purpose-built enclosed water area capable of loading and discharging vessels larger than those visiting the Port at that time. For many centuries the Town had experienced difficulties in accommodating ships, owing to the siltation of the main watercourse. The new facilities, however, overcame this problem and eventually attracted the attention of a group of railway pioneers who wished to acquire the Port as their eastern terminus.

As a result of considerable financial investment a period of substantial expansion followed. A New Dock was constructed to the north east of the Old Dock which provided increased berthing space and the ability to handle coal trains from Yorkshire and the Midlands. In addition, new traffic was attracted from Scandinavia and the Port Authority introduced a fleet of ships that established regular links with Europe.

A General View of the Royal Dock looking towards the Dock Tower during the 1920s

Although the development of the Fish Docks had a substantial impact on the Town, the Commercial Docks did not suffer as a consequence. They continued to steadily expand, resulting in the construction of an extension to the Old Dock, which created additional facilities for the handling of coal and timber. By 1879 a cutting had been excavated to allow vessels to sail directly between the two Commercial Docks without having to pass through the main entrance locks.

As Grimsby's commercial activities flourished, the need arose for a greater number of ancillary services to support visiting vessels. It was during this period that the demand for ship repairing at the Port increased. A number of new shipyards were established over the years, adjacent to the outfall to the north of the Old Dock entrance. Perhaps the most notable was J. S. Doig Limited who occupied the same site on the West Side of the Royal Dock for over fifty years.

This Company played an important role during the war years, constructing and re-fitting vessels for the Admiralty. Its location within the Dock Estate may have assisted in this, as the Port was designated a restricted area. Unfortunately the enemy had no respect for regulations and a substantial part of docks were subjected to repeated air raids. Damage was often extensive and in some cases remedial work had to be deferred until after the war.

The general development of the Port was curtailed until hostilities ceased. However, even after the war had ended there appeared to be minimal new construction work undertaken. It was not until the end of the 1950's and into the 1960's that a capital investment programme was re-introduced. This was significantly increased following the formation of the British Transport Docks Board (BTDB) in 1963.

This nationalised organisation succeeded the Docks & Inland Waterways Executive (DIWE) and the British Transport Commission (BTC) both of which had been created to operate the country's former railway ports. The BTDB committed in excess of £1.4 million to the development of the Commercial Docks between 1960 and 1971.

The level of financial investment has continued to increase particularly after privatisation in 1983. Associated British Ports (ABP) the present owner and operator has transformed Alexandra Dock following the departure of the timber tenants in the late 1970's and early 1980's. As a result of these changes, Grimsby has developed into the main northern distribution centre for the importation of Audi, Volkswagen, Seat and Skoda vehicles, together with a primary export location for Toyota cars. The Port can now provide over 125 acres (50.59 hectares) of open car storage and caters for the many car carrying vessels that regularly visit the two purpose-built roll-on/roll-off berths at the western end of Alexandra Dock.

During the past 150 years, since the Royal Dock was constructed, the Port has continued to evolve. It has had to respond to the introduction of new methods of operation including the containerisation of Danish bacon and the re-organisation of labour during the late 1980's. New cargoes attracted to the Port have often required new facilities for easier handling and storage. The various Port Authorities, over the years, have generally adopted a positive approach in meeting the needs of its customers. This has helped to ensure that Grimsby is capable of fulfilling not only present, but also future, demand. It is therefore ABP's intention to continue to build on the work that has been achieved in the past and develop the role of Grimsby's Commercial Docks in order to confidently progress forward in the 21st Century.

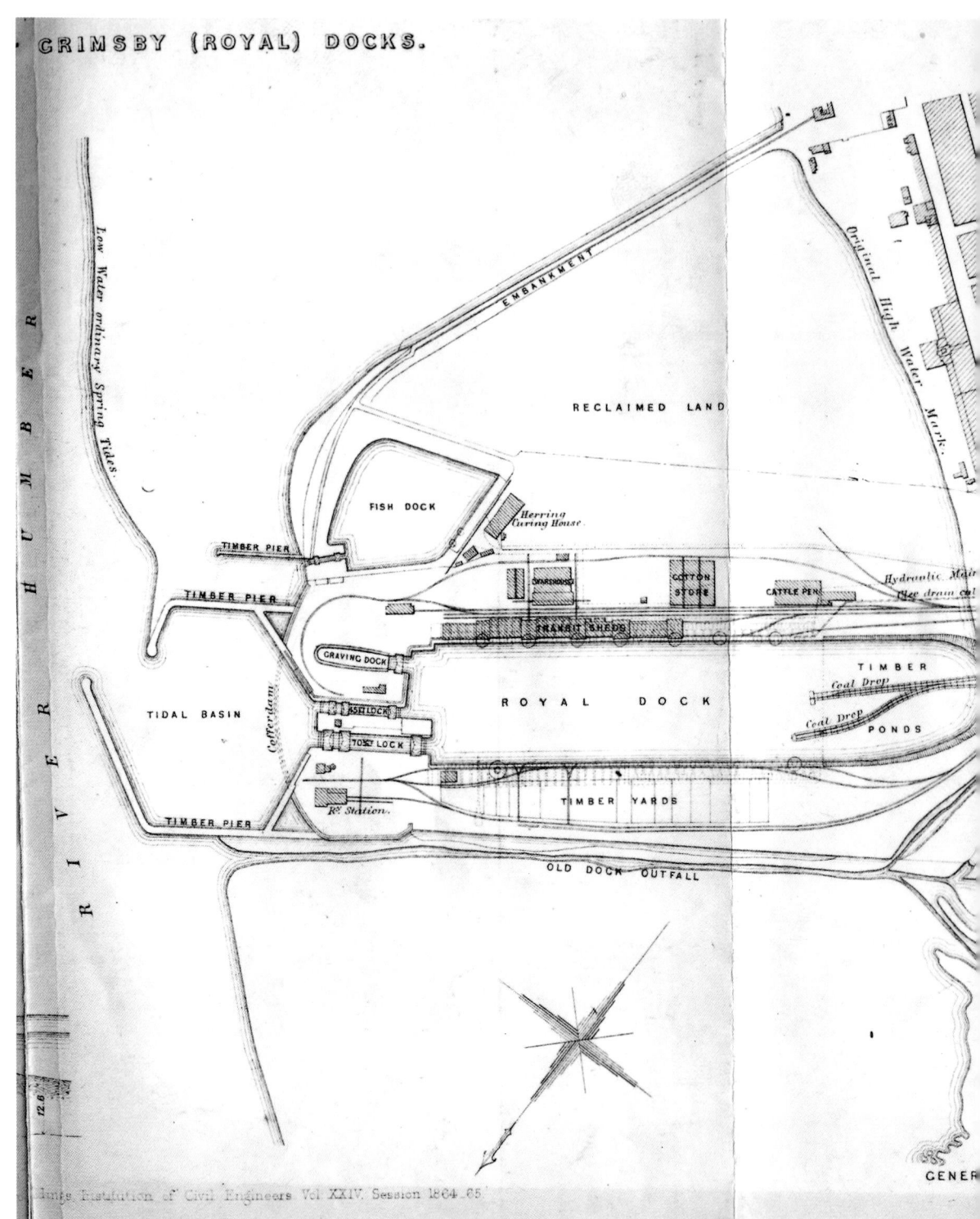

A Plan of the Old and New Docks, 1864.

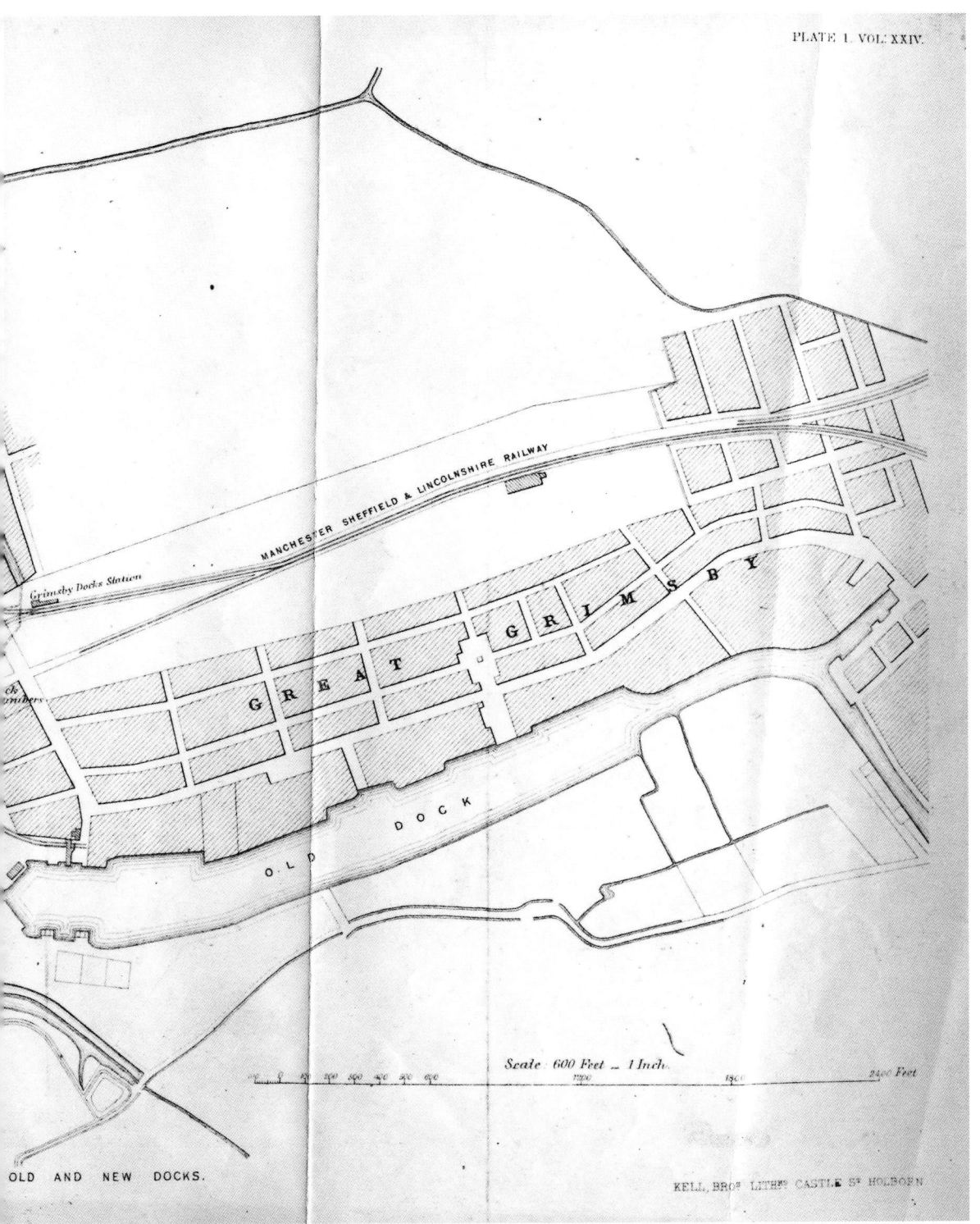

PLATE I. VOL. XXIV.

OLD AND NEW DOCKS.

KELL, BROS LITH*: CASTLE S*: HOLBORN

CHAPTER 1

The Early History of the Port

It is difficult to imagine, when travelling along Frederick Ward Way, that the adjoining River Freshney together with the River Head formed part of the original Port of Grimsby. Its origins can be traced back to at least 1165 when Henry II granted the City of Lincoln the right to raise tolls and customs against all the men from Norway who used Grimsby as a trading centre. The facilities available were extremely primitive compared with the docks of today. A small harbour had been created suitable for accommodating Scandinavian longships. In the early middle ages it was tidal to a point that is now more than a mile from the high-water mark. A small inlet from the Humber, known as the Haven, meandered across the mud flats and flowed down towards Abbey Road where, in

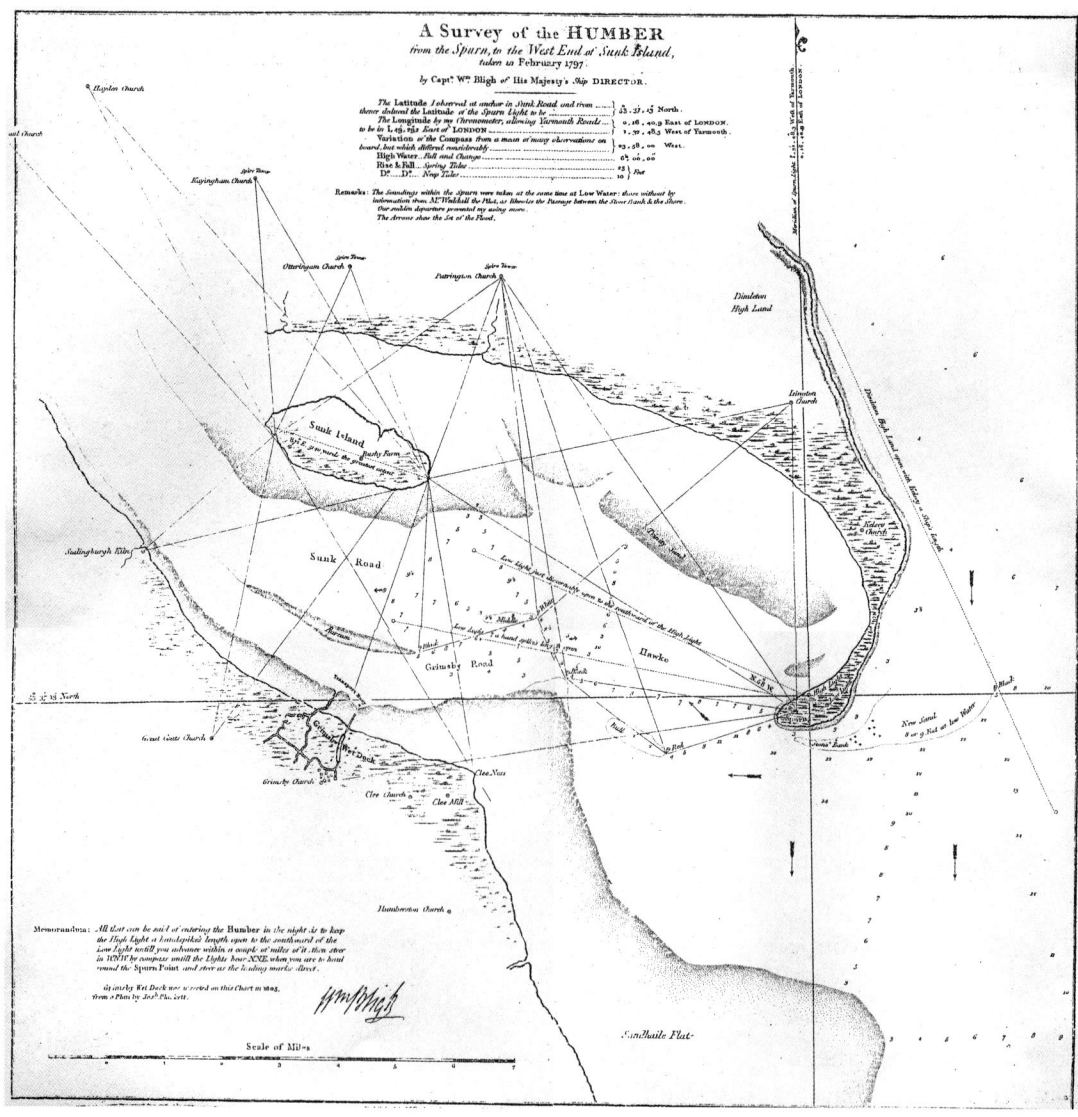

A survey of the River Humber compiled by Captain Bligh in February 1797.

1201, the Canons of Wellow had erected a water mill alongside the old haven. Shipping however, could rarely navigate beyond the present River Head.

The main foreign trade, during the early years, originated from Scandinavia when Norwegian vessels discharged their cargoes of pine and board. By 1230 this had become a regular traffic through the Port and was playing a significant part in the development of Grimsby's economy. In return the surrounding hinterland was able to provide a reasonable supply of grain, which was often harvested and exported to Norway. Whilst the business between Grimsby and Scandinavia continued to develop, the Port also experienced increasing trading links with Europe. During the 12th Century it was reported that a Flemish ship was sold in the Town and by 1228 there was evidence that Spanish merchants were starting to arrive, closely followed by the French.

Perhaps as a result of the upturn in trade, the grants of tolls to the Town awarded by Henry III in 1255 and 1261 were designed not only to allow for paving and enclosing the Borough but, more importantly, for the alteration of the Port. This potential to improve the facilities offered to visiting vessels created a sense of achievement and growth within the Town. However, the anticipated increase in prosperity of the Haven did not come to fruition and business declined as the physical condition of the facility slowly deteriorated. Although in 1280 quayage was awarded for a term of three years, complaints were already being presented before the King suggesting that shipping could not use the Haven as a result of continued silting.

In order to help overcome this problem, the Burgesses of the Borough applied for permission to divert the River Freshney so it could flow into the Haven and thereby flush away the silt. Research was undertaken at the time to determine whether there would be any detrimental effects caused by this diversion and, as a result, it was found that the site of the mill of William of Apeltrefeud, which later was known as Haven Mill, would be affected. In addition landowners and their tenants started to express concerns regarding the inaccessibility to the common in Little Coates should the course of the Freshney be altered. A further difficulty, which would no doubt have had the most adverse impact, related to the possibility of flooding at Great and Little Coates as well as the area around Laceby. In order to try and overcome this problem, it became apparent that substantial effort would be required to construct a suitable channel to divert the river. It was acknowledged that this could only be achieved by ensuring the channel was well dug and sluice gates provided. Consequently, after much thought it was decided that the river should be left intact.

Although it is acknowledged that the declining condition of the Haven may have had an adverse effect on the Town's economy, it could be questioned whether the siltation was as bad as literally interpreted. The reasoning behind this relates to reports that between 1267 and 1268, 436 quarters of corn were dispatched from Grimsby to King Edward I's forces in Flanders. These were loaded on two vessels both of which were named 'Blythe' and belonged to shipowners based in the Town. Four years later a request was made for a ship to set sail from Grimsby to join the King's forces at Berwick. In 1303 the 'Godyere', another of Grimsby's vessels, embarked upon a journey to Scotland carrying tools and bolts for use in the construction of a prefabricated bridge during Edward I's campaign of the same year. The Town was again called upon to assist the King when Edward's grandson, Edward III was on the throne. Eleven ships and 170 seamen

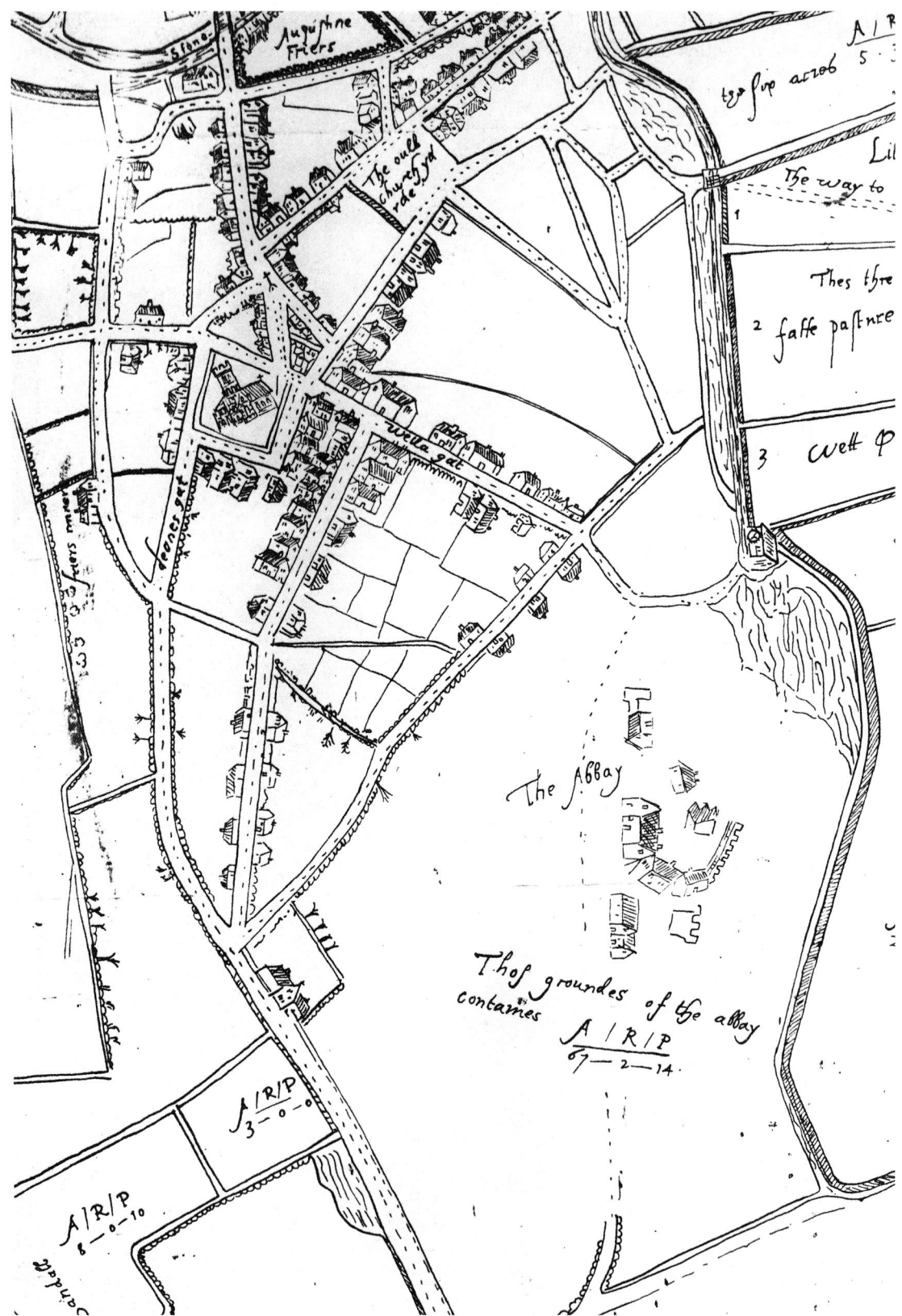

Plan of Grimsby showing the Town together with the watermill at Wellow Abbey, circa 1660.

were requested to set sail for the Siege of Calais. These activities did not really portray a port that was in the midst of a spiralling decline, as reports at the time seem to suggest.

The situation, however, did appear to change by the 16th Century as the Town was seen to be in a much poorer position than it had been for many years. The silting of the Haven was having a detrimental effect on the number of vessels using the harbour. During the early years of Queen Elizabeth I's reign, 13 ships or boats were reported as being

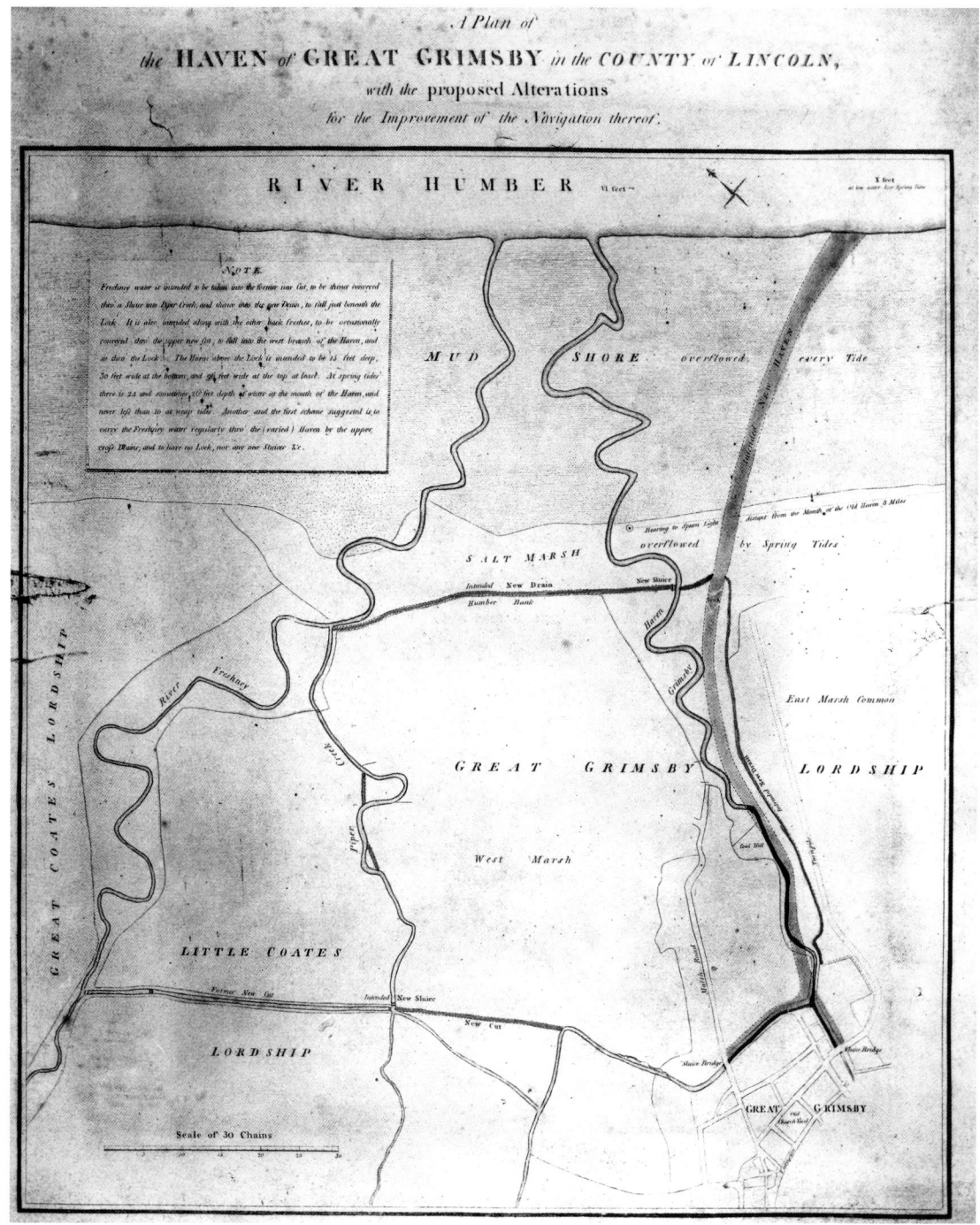

Plan accompanying the Haven Act of 1796. (ABP)

locally owned but by the 1640's this had declined to only one coal-hoy. The situation was not helped by the official assistance being provided to Hull. In 1592, the Privy Council, instructed that, between Boston and Hartlepool, no one except the merchants of Hull or those receiving the same privileges would be allowed to carry goods other than coal or mill-stones. Grimsby, however, was not unfamiliar with direct competition. During the 14th Century the Port and Borough of Ravenserod was attracting substantial trade bound for the Humber. Situated on Spurn point, a mile further east than Spurn's present position, it was ideally located to tempt passing vessels with the facilities it could offer. Although the continual loss of traffic created problems for Grimsby, it managed to overcome these difficulties and Ravenserod eventually became a victim of the eroding coastline. The dominance that was placed on Hull two centuries later was a different matter. The usual grounds associated with the competitive market failed to exist. In order to ensure that Grimsby retained its Port, it was necessary for the Town to liberally interpret the Privy Council's directive.

In attempting to protect its trading links the Borough continued to minimise the damage caused by Hull's preferential position along the East Coast. In 1638 and again in 1640 efforts were made to defend its right to collect primage in Grimsby that was being claimed by the Hull collectors. Unfortunately the continuing dominance of Hull combined with the struggle to maintain a passage along the Haven only resulted in hopeless efforts to sustain trade. By 1641, the Town, now in a state of despair, obtained letters-patent providing it with the necessary authority to solicit alms for the repair of the Haven. In order to assist in rectifying the situation, Charles I granted, in 1641, the sum of £2,500 towards the cost of repairs. The Port, however, continued to experience difficulties with siltation, the main cause of which appeared to be as a result of neglect by those living in the Town.

The assistance provided by the King did not, unfortunately, offer any permanent improvement in trade and the Port continued to decline, handling only coastwise traffic. This downward trend persisted for at least a further 19 years. By 1660, it was being reported "the creek or haven is so silted that no ship or vessel can come into the harbour, to the great decay of trade". It is surprising that the Haven was allowed to decline to such an extent, particularly as it was the third most important discharge point between the Humber and the Thames for the shipment of wool. It was also renowned for the importation of coal from the Tyne, the quantities of which were greater than those passing through the other ports along the East coast.

Charles I was not alone in providing financial support to improve the siltation problem. In 1697 Arthur Moore, one of the members of the Borough, advanced on mortgage the sum of £200 towards the cost of providing a sluice and the scouring of the Haven. On 30 June of the previous year Henry Hildiard also tried to assist the Corporation, although not financially. He gave permission to widen a ditch passing through Great Coates and redirect the Freshney into Piper's Creek in order to help scour the Haven. It was not, however, until 1700 that the Freshney was eventually diverted and the latter objective partly fulfilled. Unfortunately the benefits initially experienced following the completion of the work were only effective for a few months, as the new cut soon started to fill up. Efforts were only realistically made to overcome the silting problem when the Grimsby Haven Company was created in 1796 and work was started on the construction of the New Dock.

AN
ESTIMATE
Of the supposed Amount of the Navigation Tolls, at the under-mentioned Tonage, on the present Trade.

		Supposed Quantities.	Duty at	Total.		
			D.	L.	S.	D.
Per Quarter.	Wheat, Beans, &c.	5000	3	62	10	0
	Barley, Oats, &c.	8000	2	66	13	4
Per Chalder.	Coals,	2500	4	41	13	4
	Lime,	500	3	6	5	0
Per Ton.	Timber, Deals, Plank, &c.	500	3	5	11	2
	Groceries,	250	5	5	4	2
	Other Goods, Merchandises, &c.	750	4	12	10	0
Per Pack.	Wool,	700	2	5	16	8
				£ 206	3	8

N. B. The following Corporation-Tolls to be taken off:

Each Waggon, 2d. | Wool per Pack, 2d.
Corn per Quarter, ½d. | Hogshead, 4d.

In order to form a more certain Idea of what the Navigation may annually produce, an Account of the Turnpike-Tolls has been taken for the last 12 Years, and found to produce £2913 : 4 : 6, the Average of which is £242 : 8 : 4 per Annum, and deducting from thence the one-fifth for Chaises, Saddle-Horses, and Cattle, leaves £193 : 18 : 8. It is supposed that 13000 Quarters of Corn are yearly brought down; reckoning therefore upon an Average, 10 Quarters of Barley to a Load, then the Navigation-Toll will be 2d per Load more than the Turnpike-Toll of 18d or 4½d per Horse, for 4 Horses, which for 8000 Quarters, or 800 Loads, will give an additional Sum of £6 : 13 : 4. And reckoning a Load of Wheat upon an Average to consist of 8 Quarters, there will be 6d per Load more for the Navigation than the Turnpike, which for 5000 Quarters, or 625 Loads, will be a further Increase of £15 : 12 : 6.

It is also estimated, that 500 Tons of Timber, &c. 500 Chalders of Lime, and 2500 Chalders of Coals, are yearly brought into the Haven; and as these are principally taken back by the Waggons that bring down the Corn and Wool, and consequently pay no Toll, a further Increase may be set down of £35 for 2100 Tons at 4d, which is deducting two-fifths for what are taken by Carriages that come purposely for these Articles, and pay Toll accordingly.

Anticipated Navigation Tolls based on estimated tonnages of cargo passing through the Old Dock, dated September 1795. (ABP)

CHAPTER TWO

The Dawning of a New Era

Whilst one of the main objectives of creating a New Dock was to solve the continuing silting of the Haven, certain individuals in the Town had other intentions. They saw it as an opportunity to raise the profile of the venture and turn it into a political issue. Alderman Parker had been one of the prominent individuals to pursue this particular objective. Acting on behalf of George Tennyson, he had secretly approached Jonathan Pickernell of Whitby requesting that he prepare plans for a purpose-built Dock. Although these were completed and made available by early November 1787 they lay undisturbed until 17 December 1788, when Parker, whilst addressing a Burgess Meeting, let it be known of their existence. It would appear that this action had been specifically choreographed in order to benefit Pole and Wood, the two prospective candidates representing Tennyson's party at the forthcoming election.

Fortunately the improvement of the dock did not appear to be such a significant issue in the election campaign as originally anticipated, at least not enough to ensure the success of Tennyson's candidates. However, the matter did arise again during the year preceding the 1796 election. Tennyson and Baron Yarborough had reached a political compromise whereby their long-term differences were put to one side. This mainly came about following the death of Tennyson's uncle, Christopher Clayton, who had been opposed to Yarborough and his family. The feud between the individuals had lasted some years and in order to diffuse the situation Lord Yarborough, reluctantly, agreed that Tennyson's friend Ayscough Boucherett of North Willingham should form a joint candidature with his own nominee.

Boucherett was a leading supporter of the Haven scheme and later became the Chairman of the Haven Company. His ability to act as a mediator between Tennyson and Yarborough helped, for a time, to enable both individuals to focus their efforts on the formation of a company to progress with the dock scheme. Although Yarborough was not entirely supportive of Tennyson's proposals for the Haven scheme, he was not in a position to oppose it as joint action was required if it was to receive Parliamentary Approval. In addition, a united approach was essential as opponents based in Hull were already mobilising their efforts to bring pressure upon the Treasury to prevent the passing of the Bill. It was obvious that Hull did not wish Grimsby to develop its facilities, as it could become a direct threat to its almost monopolistic operations on the Humber. J. S. Brandstrom, a sympathetic Hull merchant, highlighted this situation when he stated that the Dock Company in Hull, Trinity House and the Corporation would make every effort to oppose the proposed improvements. Hull had realised that the potential existed for Grimsby to have a detrimental effect upon its trade.

Despite the opposition to the expansion of the Haven, Grimsby continued to progress with its plans. As part of his proposals Pickernell had put forward a large project that would include the provision of 6,270 yards (5,733 metres) of quay space costing an estimated £52,357. This length of quay was unheard of at the time and would indicate the foresight he must have possessed when designing the New Dock. The whole scheme required the removal of no less than 1,767,128 cubic yards (1,351,146 cubic metres) of clay and soil which, when excavated to a depth of 18 feet (5.49 metres), would create an area of approximately 60 acres (24.28 hectares). Calculated at four pence per cubic yard this part of the project would have cost £29,452 and, when combined with the provision of warehouses together with contingencies and the engineer's percentage, the total cost of the scheme was estimated to be in the region of £125,000.

Although the plans provided great opportunities for increased trade from the Baltic, they, together with the Bill outlining the proposed works, started to cause some anxiety. This was mainly concerned with the possibility of flooding to the West of the Town. Mr. G. Watkinson, a landowner of Southwell, writing to George Babb in March 1796, referred to the silting up of the Freshney. Robert Newton Lee also communicating with Babb, in February 1796, stated that, "if the present plan is carried into execution part of my estate at Little Coates will be liable to be

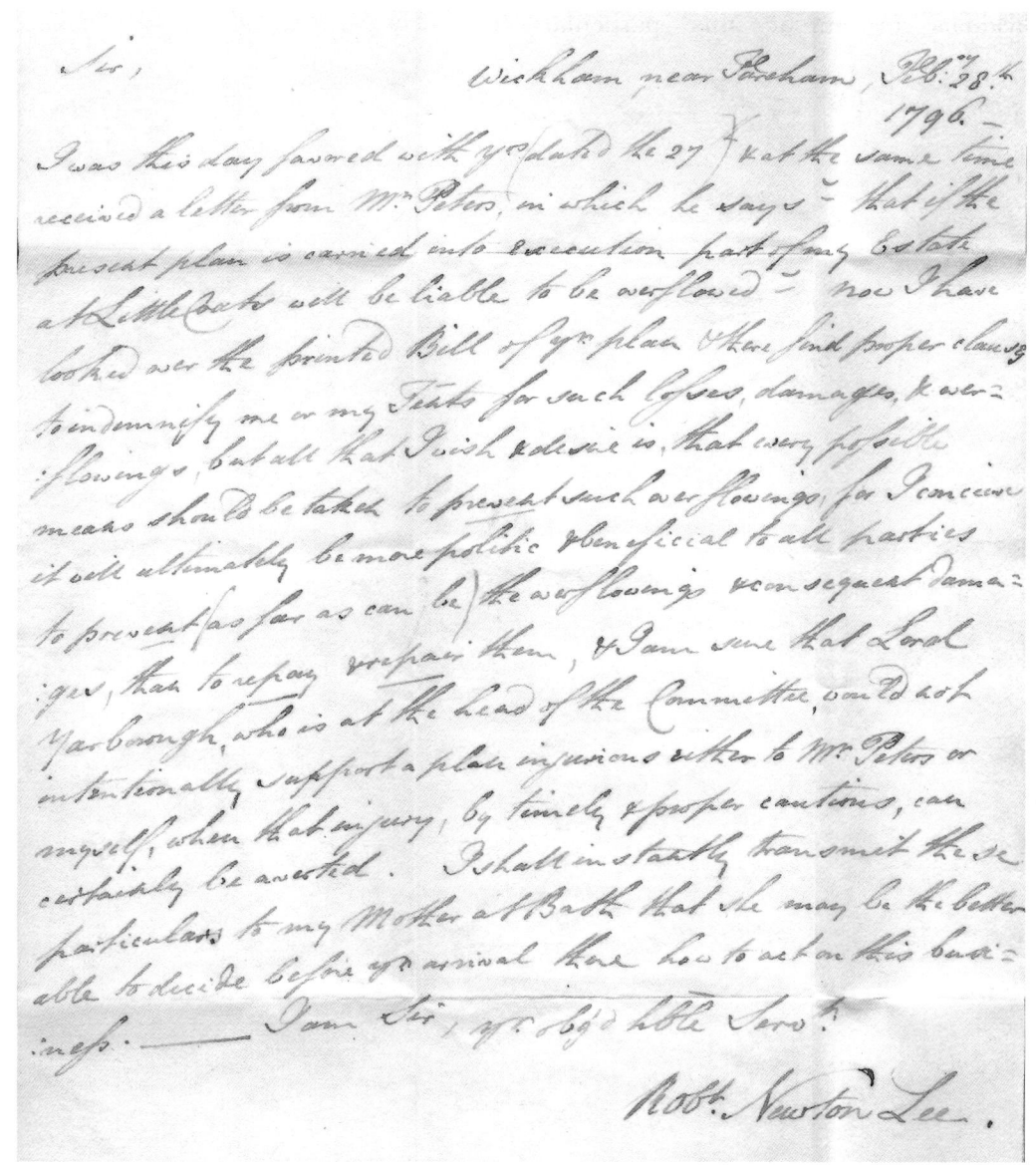

Letter from Mr. Robert Newton Lee, Landowner at Littlecoates, to Mr. George Babb dated 27 February 1796. (ABP)

overflowed". It would appear that, unlike the situation in 1280 when the diversion of the Freshney was originally suggested, clauses had now been included in the Bill to indemnify the landowners and their tenants for any losses or damages in respect of flooding. However, it is evident from Mr. Newton Lee's correspondence that the main priority for the landowners was to receive assurance that "every possible means should be taken to prevent such overflowings".

Despite the reservations of the landowners and their tenants, the Bill passed through Parliament receiving Royal Assent and becoming the Grimsby Haven Act in 1796. The Act provided the necessary authority to allow for the widening, enlarging, altering and improving of the Haven. Part of the funding for the work was to be received in the form of a subsidy from the Government in return for Naval vessels using the new Port's facilities. Pickernell was of the opinion that "all ships of war, if in want of water or provisions, will naturally come to Grimsby sooner than go to Hull". To support this theory he had taken the trouble to forward copies of his plans to Trinity House, London and the Treasury before despatching them to Grimsby. This gave him the opportunity to notify the relevant authorities of the potential improvements that were being considered for the Town, in the hope that regular Naval support would become a reality. The ability to accommodate Naval vessels would, however, not be an entirely new practice as they had called at Grimsby in the past. On one occasion in 1739, it was reported that the Captain of the H.M.S. 'Salamander' had thought it advantageous to land a press gang in order to recruit local "volunteers". During another instance the lieutenant of the 'Greenwich' berthed his vessel and presented a warrant before the Mayor in order to arrest deserters who were seeking refuge in the Town.

Unfortunately, Pickernell did not receive overwhelming local support for his proposals. George Babb, the Town Clerk, being largely responsible for the formation of the Grimsby Haven Company and a prominent campaigner for a New Dock, had a distinct dislike for spending money. He felt that Pickernell's project was perhaps a little too costly, and after reading an article in Phillips "History of the Inland Navigation" had the misguided belief that he was a Civil Engineer. This resulted in him favouring a smaller scheme drawn up in 1794 by John Hudson of Kenwick Thorpe, one of Lincolnshire's leading surveyors.

After lengthy debate and obvious superiority in preparing realistic plans for the dock, Pickernell was appointed engineer for the works. Although this was regarded as a personal achievement, the capital authorised by the Haven Act, £20,000 with a further £10,000 in reserve, had been based on estimates provided by Hudson and proved completely inadequate for the work now in hand. As a result, the Company soon found itself in financial difficulties and inevitable changes had to be made. The Committee responsible for the works started to amend the plans as time progressed and it was not long before it became untenable for Pickernell to remain as its engineer. This was the revenge George Babb had been seeking but his cavalier attitude towards the plans, together with his contempt for Civil Engineers, appeared to reflect the general outlook of the Company, which in turn grossly underestimated the difficulties that lay ahead.

Before the work could commence, various requirements, as determined by the Act, had to be fulfilled. It had become apparent that the East Marsh common land bordering the New Dock would become inaccessible should the Mayor and Burgesses of the Town lease the area for dockside development. In order to overcome this problem it was stipulated that three common staiths should be provided from the turnpike, now Victoria Street, to the quayside. These were to be for public use and measure ten yards (9.14 metres) in width in respect of "Ranters Wharf" (A) (between MFI building and the bus depot) and "Lower Staiths Wharf" (C) (between Albert Gaits and Curry's buildings), whilst "Freeport Wharf" (B) (the main approach to Corporation Bridge) would be restricted to eight yards (7.32 metres) in width. Once these rights of way had been provided, the remaining 16 acres (6.48 hectares) of land between the Haven and the turnpike could be made available for the erection of warehouses and other buildings adjacent to the New Dock.

Aerial view of the Old Dock, later to be renamed Alexandra Dock showing the location of the three staiths. (NELC Local Studies Library)

CHAPTER THREE

Creating the First Enclosed Dock in the Town

Following the completion of the legal requirements of the Act steps could then be taken to proceed with the construction work, but the departure of Jonathan Pickernell had left the project without a resident engineer. It was thought that Alderman Lusby, a local builder and general "Jack of all Trades" could suitably fill the vacancy and supervise the work. Babb was under the impression that the work carried out by Civil Engineers was far too costly and the plans, particularly those put forward by Pickernell, were of a "grand design". His attitude was that "any man of common sense without pretending to be an engineer must see in a moment that half of them are superfluous".

This arrogant stance adopted by George Babb did not help to improve the situation when Alderman Lusby advised Ralph Tennyson that part of the navigation below the lock had slipped into the channel as a result of recent heavy rains. Rather than employ a resident engineer or consult Pickernell's assistant, Michael Pilley of Lincoln, the Company acted in its usual manner. A group of four members, headed by the Mayor, decided to inspect the problem and as a result recommended that digging should continue to increase the depth by a further two feet. It was hoped that by adopting this approach "the effects of the slips would be fully seen". Lusby, however, was not convinced that this would be the correct action to take and urged Tennyson to contact Pilley before any further damage could be caused.

The main problem appeared to be associated with the geology of the area. The rock into which piles could be secured was too deep and the composition of the clay changed with depth. If trial borings or cuts had been made it may have highlighted potential concerns and the necessary action could have been taken. In finding the consistency of the clay had changed, Lusby was caught unawares and this may have prompted many of the members of the Company to become seriously concerned about the events of the first year.

The continual digging and re-digging of the Haven soon saw the funds decrease and the situation was not helped by problems experienced with the contractors. The main excavation work was awarded to Jonathan Scutt of Walling Fen, Howden, Yorkshire, and his partner, Henry Walker of Lincoln. Whilst Scutt appeared ready to start work, Walker had difficulties in finding sureties for his £500 bond and was discharged from his responsibilities in December 1796 "having also misconducted himself in the prosecution and management of the said work". Finding he no longer had a partner, Scutt was either unable or unwilling to fulfil the contract and decided, a month later, to buy himself out. This created extreme difficulties for Lusby who had to let the digging work wherever possible.

Continually confronted with rapidly rising costs and depleting financial resources, the Committee decided in February 1797 that a smaller lock should be constructed, thereby reducing its original length by 126 feet (38.40 metres). At the same time the Committee was granted the authority to consult an engineer, which enabled the services of John Rennie to be engaged without delay. He travelled to

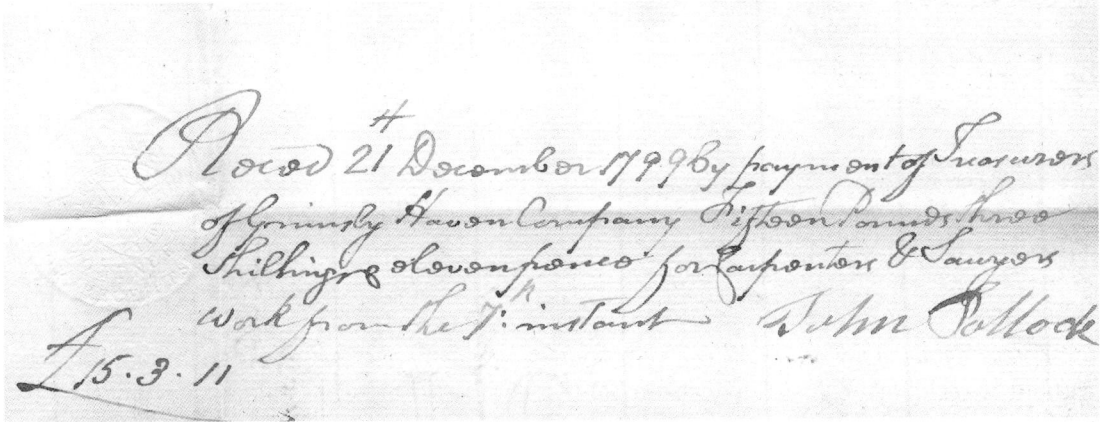

Receipt for the sum of £15 3s 11d (£15.19) in respect of Carpenters and Sawyers work undertaken for the Haven Company, dated 21 December 1799. (ABP)

Grimsby on 5 June 1797 and after inspecting the plans prepared a report that was made available to the Committee a month later. It would appear that Rennie did not recommend any change to the plans and was not therefore invited to become resident engineer.

However, the situation was to change. The construction works experienced two substantial disasters in quick succession. Despite undertaking precautionary piling, the lock works were "blown" on 20 August and two days later the walls at the southern end of the lock slipped causing grave concern to all those involved in the work. The shareholders were looking to place the blame but Lusby, writing to Tennyson, concluded "I shall content myself with having acted strictly according to the plans laid down by the diffr. Engineers". Whilst Rennie was consulted with regard to the problems, it was not until 15 February 1798 that he was formally invited to become the Company's engineer. A month after his appointment his assistant, George Joyce was contracted to supervise the work at a salary of 150 guineas.

Although the work under the control of Rennie and Joyce was seen as an improvement on their predecessors it was not long before Joyce fell out of favour. Siltation was still causing a problem and with debts continuing to increase, the Committee declared that the employment of those involved in the digging work would cease. Carpenters and Smiths, however, would be retained in order to finish the lock gates.

The financial situation had to be resolved and in January 1800 Babb announced proposals instigated by John Pickerton to call in a further £9,000. Plans and specifications laid down by Rennie to complete the project required a sum of £6,901. This figure had to be increased by an additional £2,000 to cover the outstanding debts. The Company tried to save money, but the drastic economies it made had an adverse effect on the main dock structures, including the pier, the apron and the return wing walls. Rennie decided to express his opposition to the proposals by indicating that if the apron was removed he could not ensure the safety of the lock for one week. He went on to state that without the piers or a suitable alternative of equal value, the fear existed whereby the water would get behind the return tail wings of the lock resulting in the possible emptying of the dock.

The Committee was dissatisfied with the situation and already being out of favour, Joyce was blamed for the troubles that had occurred. He was replaced in May 1800 by one of Rennie's principal assistants James

Hollingsworth, who travelled to the Town in time to witness another partial collapse of the wing walls. The structure had been too heavy for the insecure foundations and Hollingsworth had little option but to dismantle them immediately.

These problems appeared to be the last in the construction of the Dock. However, whilst it is reported that the Company ordered it to be opened on 30 December 1800, no goods at all were imported during the following year. It could therefore be concluded that the celebrations held by the ringing of St James' bells together with the banquet attended by distinguished guests, may have been to mark its completion rather than its opening. It would appear that the Dock was formally open for business in November 1801 and that the final cost of the project, by the time the Company had seriously considered its total expenditure in 1813, amounted to £68,940.

The original Lock Pit entrance to the Old Dock, circa 1840. (NELC Local Studies Library)

CHAPTER FOUR

The Demise of the Grimsby Haven Company

The scheme devised at the end of the 18th Century had finally come to fruition. A purpose-built dock covering an area of 15 acres (6.07 hectares), complete with an entrance lock measuring 150 feet (45.72 metres) in length by 37 feet (11.28 metres) wide with a depth of 18 feet (5.49 metres) of water on the sill at high tide, had been created in approximately five years. Although there was great expectation in the Town as a result of its opening, the facilities available were rather poor in comparison to those provided at Hull or Goole. Part of the work had still to be completed. The piers had not been constructed and the present condition of the lock was unable to adequately maintain a sufficient water level within the Dock. Perhaps these inefficiencies could explain the slow start in securing trade that was being experienced at the time.

It was not until 1802 that the New Dock started handling imports. The first reports related to the expected arrival of 800 tons (812.8 tonnes) of iron, most of which may have been used in construction projects taking place in the Town. In addition, approximately 647 hundreds of deals together with 967 consignments of timber were seen to be the main trade for that year. Whilst it had always been acknowledged that Grimsby would be an importation centre, the aforementioned cargoes could not have been realistically regarded as an encouraging start to the operation. Fortunately between 1803 and 1805 trade increased and the income from dues rose from £480 in 1802 to £934 in 1805. This was also reflected in the number of vessels visiting the Port, which by 1805 had reached 67, totalling 17,792 tons (18,076.7 tonnes).

During 1805 Ayscough Boucheret, Chairman of the Haven Company, prepared a descriptive document highlighting the attributes of the "New Wet Dock at Grimsby".

A

DESCRIPTION

OF THE

NEW WET DOCK

AT GRIMSBY,

IN THE COUNTY OF LINCOLN.

1805.

THE ancient Port of GRIMSBY, in the county of Lincoln, which, in the reign of Elizabeth, ranked amongst the first in the North of England, having had, for many years, its Haven nearly choaked up: a number of Gentlemen, conceiving from the local advantages it possessed, and that by fixing Flood and Ebb Gates, with Sluices, a Wet Dock might be made of almost any requisite capacity, and the outfal be kept permanently open, entered into a Subscription for raising a competent sum of money; and in 1796 obtained an Act of Parliament for enlarging and improving the Haven. In the execution of this laudable undertaking they have expended £60,000 and upwards; and constituting, as they now do, an Incorporated Company, they offer to the Public, through the medium of their Chairman, the following brief description of the local and improved situation of the place.

The Haven of Grimsby is situated somewhat more than seven miles from the mouth of the great river Humber, in about a west direction from the Spurn Lights; and in the approach thereto there are no risks to encounter from a Bar Harbour, or a tedious and dangerous River Navigation.

The Lock, within the Haven, is about a quarter of a mile from the Humber, and is one of the most capacious in England; its dimensions being one hundred and fifty feet in length, and its width at the top thirty-eight feet.

The Depth of Water at the lowest Neap Tides is 12 feet.
———————— at ordinary Spring ditto   20 do.
———————— at great Spring ditto   23 do.

The Ebb Gates pen up, to a certain extent, eighteen feet depth of water; further within the Dock, fifteen feet; and from thence to the extremities by the sides of the town, which are at a distance of upwards of half a mile, fourteen feet. The whole excavation is above fifteen acres, and is capable of containing two hundred sail of ships or upwards, allowing each sufficient room for loading and discharging. Adjoining to the Bason, at the entrance of the Wet Dock, there are also constructed Carpenters' Ways, a Dry Dock, Building Yard, &c. of considerable extent, for the conveniency of graving and repairing ships.

The front page of a three-page document prepared by Mr. A. Boucheret, Chairman of the Haven Company, detailing the facilities together with Rates and Duties of the New Dock, dated February 1805. (ABP)

Despite his gallant efforts to promote the benefits of the new facilities, the prosperous fortunes of the Port did not continue. By the following year inward shipping had declined by just under 50% to 37 vessels. Basic imports of iron, deals and timber were down to 46 tons, 472 hundred and 2,076 consignments respectively. The situation should have improved after the great Baltic trade freeze of 1808, but this did not happen. By 1811, a decade after the Dock was opened, imports were recorded as being a mere 5,413 tons (5,499.6 tonnes). The next ten years did reflect a noticeable improvement, but by 1819/1820 it had only reached 5,988 tons (6,083.8 tonnes).

The merchants who had initially promoted Grimsby as an import centre during the early years, were now finding that the immediate hinterland had little produce to export. This meant that, unlike today when vessels can discharge and load cargoes during the same visit, ships of the 19th Century were only calling at the Port with inward-bound commodities. Coastal trade was experiencing a similar situation with only 37 coasters calling at Grimsby during 1823.

The failure of the Port's development was highlighted when compared with the fortunes of Goole. During 1828 Goole's coastwise traffic averaged 1,240, rising to 1,619 vessels in 1834. It is, however, perhaps unfair to compare the two ports as Goole had established excellent communications with the industrial heartlands of Yorkshire by means of the Aire & Calder Canal. Whilst Grimsby had a better geographical location, having a shorter sailing time from the North Sea, the Town could not offer any means of transporting goods over a substantial distance to or from the Dock.

The Port started to enter a period of stagnation. Sufficient trade could not be attracted to prevent the Haven Company seeing the debt to its annuitants rise to £30,000 by 1810. The capital cost, calculated

Commercial barges regularly visited the River Head to load and discharge their cargoes, many of which either originated or were destined for the adjoining tenants.

South Arm, Alexandra Dock, looking north with floating timber in the foreground and the Dock Tower which can be faintly seen to the left of the chimney. (NELC Local Studies Library)

in 1800 to be approximately £68,000, increased to £204,000. This additional expenditure had occurred as a direct result of the non-payment of various financial obligations amounting to £136,000 that had accumulated over a forty-six year period.

The Company, by the 1840's, was experiencing severe financial problems and there was little to indicate how long the Port could survive without the introduction of a suitable communication system to support its facilities. It was therefore fortunate that the Sheffield, Ashton-under-Lyne & Manchester Railway Company had been seeking to establish a terminus on the East Coast. During September 1844 it began negotiations with Lord Worsley, the Chairman of the Haven Company with a view to entering an agreement to take over the operation of the Port.

Meanwhile a group of local landowners gathered at the Red Lion Hotel in Caistor on 28 October 1844 to discuss proposals presented by a group of Sheffield businessmen to build a railway to Grimsby. They had suggested that a connection be provided to the Town from the proposed Sheffield & Lincolnshire Junction Railway that was terminating at Gainsborough. At a second meeting held eight days later at the Town Hall in Grimsby three possible routes were put forward for discussion. After some deliberation it was decided to pursue the route that would pass through Brigg covering a distance of 36.5 miles from Grimsby to Gainsborough. Although the route via Caistor was the shortest at 34.75 miles, together with the route via Market Rasen, it was dismissed. The new railway was to be known as the Great

The Dock Master's House on the West Side of the original lock entrance of the Old Dock, 1873. (Cosalt)

The main approach to the Old Dock serves as the last resting place for this vessel. The water from the sluice laps around the hull before making its way towards the Humber. The two knuckles forming the entrance to the original lock can clearly be seen on either side of the creek. In the background stands the ready mixed concrete plant, adjacent to Alexandra Dock, operated by Tarmac Topmix Limited. (David Cowell)

Grimsby & Sheffield Junction Railway (GG&SJ) and by the end of 1844 it had come to an agreement with the Grimsby Haven Company to create the Grimsby Docks Company.

As part of the Haven Act of 1796 the Haven Company had acquired statutory obligations in connection with the running of the Port. The creation of a new company to fulfil these obligations could not, therefore, just be formed as a matter of course. Procedures had to be put in place to arrange for the transfer, which resulted in a Bill being placed before Parliament to effect the change-over. The Dock Act was passed in 1845 authorising not only the purchase of the existing Dock and the transfer of responsibilities, but also the construction of a new dock on land to be reclaimed from the Humber. Whilst this new legislation had created the opportunity for the Port to develop, it had resulted in the demise of the Grimsby Haven Company.

The construction of the railway into Grimsby was also progressing well. The Act of Parliament required to proceed with the building of the GG&SJ received Royal Assent on 30 June 1845. However, the Town was not

just acquiring one railway but two, as the East Lincolnshire Railway (ELR) had presented plans to connect Grimsby, Louth and Boston with the Great Northern Railway (GNR) which, at that time, was known as the London & York. The building of this connection to the South received Parliamentary Approval on the same day as the GG&SJ was granted permission to construct its branch lines to Barton and Cleethorpes. It was suggested, before the Act was passed, that the ELR join with the GG&SJ in the proposed formation of the Manchester Sheffield & Lincolnshire Railway (MS&L). When the Amalgamation Act received Royal Assent on 27 July 1846 the ELR was not included, but this did not prevent the MS&L offering the Company the opportunity to work and lease the line from Boston into Grimsby. The GNR, however, realised the potential that could be achieved if it could establish its own links with the Town. As a result of negotiations with the ELR the two companies eventually reached an agreement on 4 February 1847 to form a working relationship, thereby providing a direct link between Grimsby and the South.

Barges congregate at the rear of Marshall's Mill waiting to discharge their cargoes of grain. The timber tenancies on the west side of Alexandra Dock can be seen in the background. (NELC Local Studies Library)

CHAPTER FIVE

The Construction of the New Dock

Both of the main Railway Companies running into Grimsby started their operations on 1st March 1848. The MS&L had laid a track to New Holland whilst the Great Northern had established a route from Grimsby to Louth. It was now possible for the two Companies to provide, on a 50/50 basis, a direct service from Louth to Hull via one of the two paddle steamers newly acquired by the MS&L. This new railway system had created a great deal of excitement in the Town, the majority of which seems to have been directed towards the MS&L. This perhaps is not surprising as the Company had also started, through its amalgamation with the Grimsby Dock Company, to identify a location for a new dock as part of its expansion programme for the existing Port.

James Rendell had already prepared plans, prior to the granting of the Grimsby Dock and the MS&L Acts of 1845. The Company was therefore in an extremely advantageous position when the amalgamation of the individual railway organisations together with the Grimsby Dock Company was approved as part of the MS&L Railway (Amalgamation) Act of 1846.

The design put forward not only concentrated on the provision of a new enclosed dock but also catered for the creation of a large graving dock, a small dock for the berthing of fishing vessels, two entrance locks, a tidal basin, and an area of substantial size for the use as a timber pond. As part of the new facilities great emphasis had been placed on the fact that the enlarged Port could allow passage to ships at all times. In order to satisfy this objective it was acknowledged that the dock would have to be constructed beyond the low water mark. This was not going to be an easy task, as it would involve reclaiming a substantial part of the foreshore from the river. This could only be achieved by advancing three quarters of a

The first train operated by the Manchester, Sheffield & Lincolnshire Railway passing under Deansgate Bridge, 1 March 1848. (Illustrated London News)

mile out into the Humber beyond the entrance of the existing Dock. Once the scale of undertaking the project had been appreciated work could then commence on the construction of the cofferdam, embankments and wharves. Rendell together with his resident engineer, Adam Smith of Brigg, started work during the Spring of 1846 and by the end of 1848 the cofferdam together with the embankments were completed, thereby providing a totally enclosed area in which the New Dock could be excavated.

Whilst there was great enthusiasm to progress with the work, the sinking of the first pile could have been the last. The fact that the pile was totally lost in the underlying quicksand resulted in difficulties the contractors had not previously foreseen. In view of these problems envious neighbours remarked with selfish glee, "There is the end to the Grimsby Dock". This thought was only founded on a wish and, as we have seen, has proved a failure as a prophecy. Instead of feeling despondent, Rendell and his team set to work and, although the quicksand absorbed hundreds of tons of chalk, the

structure started to take shape.

The cofferdam extended 1,500 feet (457.2 metres) in front of the site and consisted of two arcs with a return on the western side. In view of the fact that it was located out in the river, which had a flow of seven knots together with a rise and fall of 25 feet (7.62 metres) on spring tides, it had to be well supported and of great strength. The subsoil, however, was not of firm consistency as it generally comprised of a top layer of soft, blue, silky clay averaging 24 feet (7.32 metres) in depth. The underlying strata was little better as its composition included two and a half feet of leaves and peat, a seam of sand and gravel, a layer of stiff brown clay measuring approximately 30 feet (9.14 metres) in thickness and a band of green sand mixed with water two feet wide. A firm chalk base was located between 80 (24.38 metres) and 100 feet (30.48 metres) below the surface and could therefore have only been exposed if the contractor had excavated down to this level.

The cofferdam was constructed by arranging three rows of Memel fir timber piles across the entrance of the future Dock. The

The construction of the New Dock showing the semi-circular cofferdam extending out into the river together with the two adjoining wharves, circa 1848. (Illustrated London News)

Construction work on the New Dock looking north, with sailing ships entering the Old Dock in the background to the left of the photograph, circa 1849. (ABP)

front row was located seven feet from the middle row, which in turn was spaced six feet from the back row. Each pile, depending upon its position within the three separate rows, measured between 37 (11.28 metres) to 60 feet (18.29 metres) in length, by 14 to 16 inches square (35.56 to 40.64 centimetres).

To assist in securing the whole structure, all the piles were attached together with iron fasteners and a compound of the best selected clay, combined with gravel or small amounts of broken chalk, was placed between each row to a height of five feet. This mixture was further solidified by adopting a practice of tipping the infill direct from rail wagons running over the top of the dam. The joints of the front row of piles were also caulked and pitched to the highest water mark at spring tides in order to ensure the water of the Humber did not seep into the construction area.

On either side of the dam two wharves were built. The one to the west, which lay alongside the main approach to the Old Dock, measured 2,431 feet (740.97 metres) in length whilst the other to the east was only 1,208

feet (348.20 metres) to the adjoining embankment. The latter was constructed of a single row of Memel fir sheet piles averaging between 35 (10.67 metres) and 40 feet (12.19 metres) in length. Unfortunately the stability of the ground to the east had a great deal to be desired and it was necessary to deposit layers of chalk to improve its composition.

Once the wharves, cofferdam and embankments had been completed it was possible to commence with the main excavation work. The enclosed area was drained using two 35 horse power engines but the work was not without its problems. A number of fresh water springs were discovered during the removal of the clay, which seriously placed at risk the safety of the foundations. The situation was resolved by the main contractor, Messrs. Hutching, Brown & Wright under the supervision of Rendell.

The Dock was designed to be entered by one of two locks located either side of a central island measuring 70 feet (21.34 metres) in width. The lock to the west was the larger of the two being 300 feet (91.44 metres) long between the inner and outer lock gates and 70 feet (21.34 metres) wide. The smaller lock measured only 200 feet (60.96 metres) in length by 45 feet (13.72 metres) in width. This part of the project required considerable resources to achieve. Excluding the sheeting piles, 6,180 timber piles, mainly of English elm and Scottish fir were driven to form the foundations of the locks, central pier and wing walls. This equated to in excess of 254,000 cubic feet (7188.20 cubic metres) of timber being used in this area of the Dock alone. Although both locks still remain, a decision was made in the 1970's to construct a roadway across the mouth of the smaller lock restricting its use to a layby berth only.

The water was retained in the Dock by the use of two pairs of ebb-gates, and one pair of flood-gates which controlled the amount of water allowed into the Dock at high water on spring tides. The ebb-gates, also referred to as the outer and inner gates, allowed vessels to enter the Dock when the level of water in the river was lower than that in the Dock. The timber for their construction was chiefly oak

from the Black Forest but teak and mahogany were also used as a result of the difficulty in obtaining sound oak for the scantlings. Each leaf of the flood-gates of the 70 feet (21.56 metres) lock measured 32 feet (9.75 metres) in height from the bottom of the lowest bar to the upper surface of the top bar. Their total width amounted to 84 feet (25.60 metres), each leaf measuring 42 feet (12.80 metres) from the back of the heel post to the front of the mitre post and weighing approximately 75 tons (76.2 tonnes). At the time of construction these gates were regarded as the largest that had ever been erected.

The gates were designed to work using hydraulic pressure gained from a tank of water located 200 feet (60.96 metres) above the ground in the adjacent Dock Tower. The water was forced into the tank by two 10-inch force pumps, which were worked by a duplicate 25 horse power horizontal engine. The gates were opened and closed by an endless chain that was set in motion using piston rods passing through both ends of three large cylinders. The main cylinder was

A view from the East Pier looking towards the two lock entrances with the Dock Master's House and original Dock Station to the right of the photograph. (Chris Turner)

placed on the centre pier or island whilst the remaining two were on the outer sides of each lock. They were arranged so that they could be operated by hand should the hydraulic machinery fail. The chains were linked and worked using toothed wheels in conjunction with drums onto which the gate chains were attached. Each drum was equipped with disconnecting gear and a brake in order to release it from the toothed wheel should the need arise. The cost of providing the lock gate operating machinery for both locks, including the foundations and cast iron pits for the chains, amounted to £4,000. The system was considered to be so efficient that it required only two individuals to man the gates at each lock, which were capable of being opened in two and a half minutes.

An area to the East of the small lock had been designated for the construction of a Graving Dock. Although this structure was not completed until after the main Dock was opened, its provision had been included in the original plans. During the principal building works a chalk rubble masonry dam had been

placed across the north eastern corner of the Dock. This temporary blockade was eventually removed to reveal the entrance to the Graving Dock. Measuring 70 feet (21.34metres) in width it could be sealed by closing two gates similar in construction to the ebb-gates across the larger of the two locks. This then allowed the water to be pumped out of the Graving Dock leaving the enclosed vessels within a dry environment. Behind these gates the dry dock extended 350 feet (106.68 metres) northwards and formed a structure that measured 96 feet (29.26 metres) across at a point where it was level with the surrounding land, tapering downwards to 52 feet (15.85 metres) at its base. The Dock was designed by Adam Smith and constructed at a cost of £32,000 by James Taylor of Manchester under the supervision of Edward Hele Clark. It was formally opened on 8 June 1858 and the first vessel to be accommodated within this new facility was the 1200 ton steam packet 'Atlantic' from Hull.

The walls of the main Dock were formed primarily of long piers with brick arching

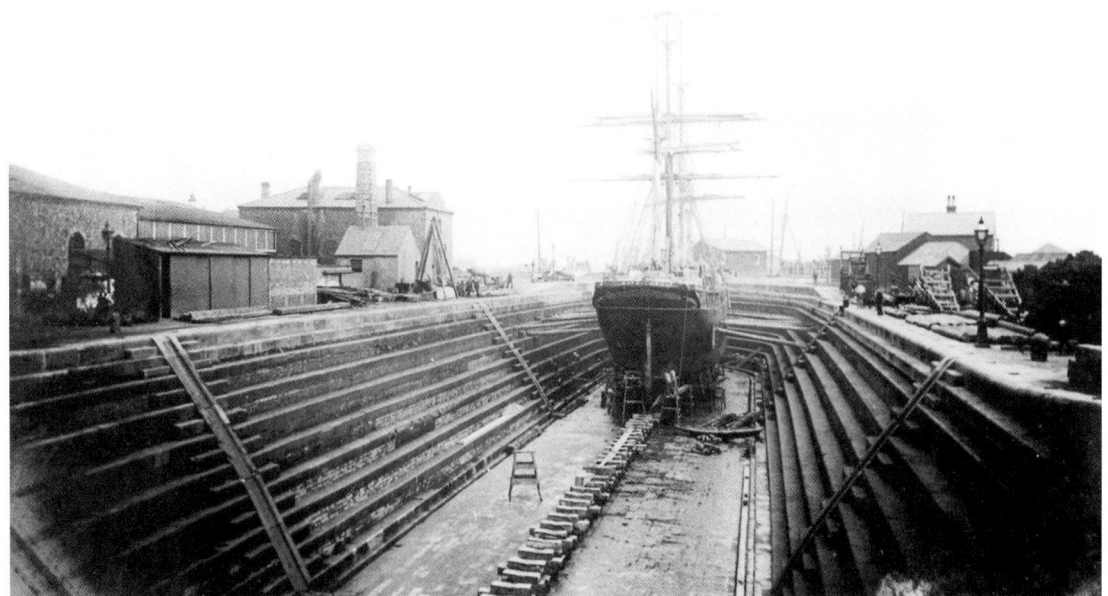

A sailing ship undergoing repair work within the confines of the Graving Dock, during the early 1900's. (NELC Welholme Galleries)

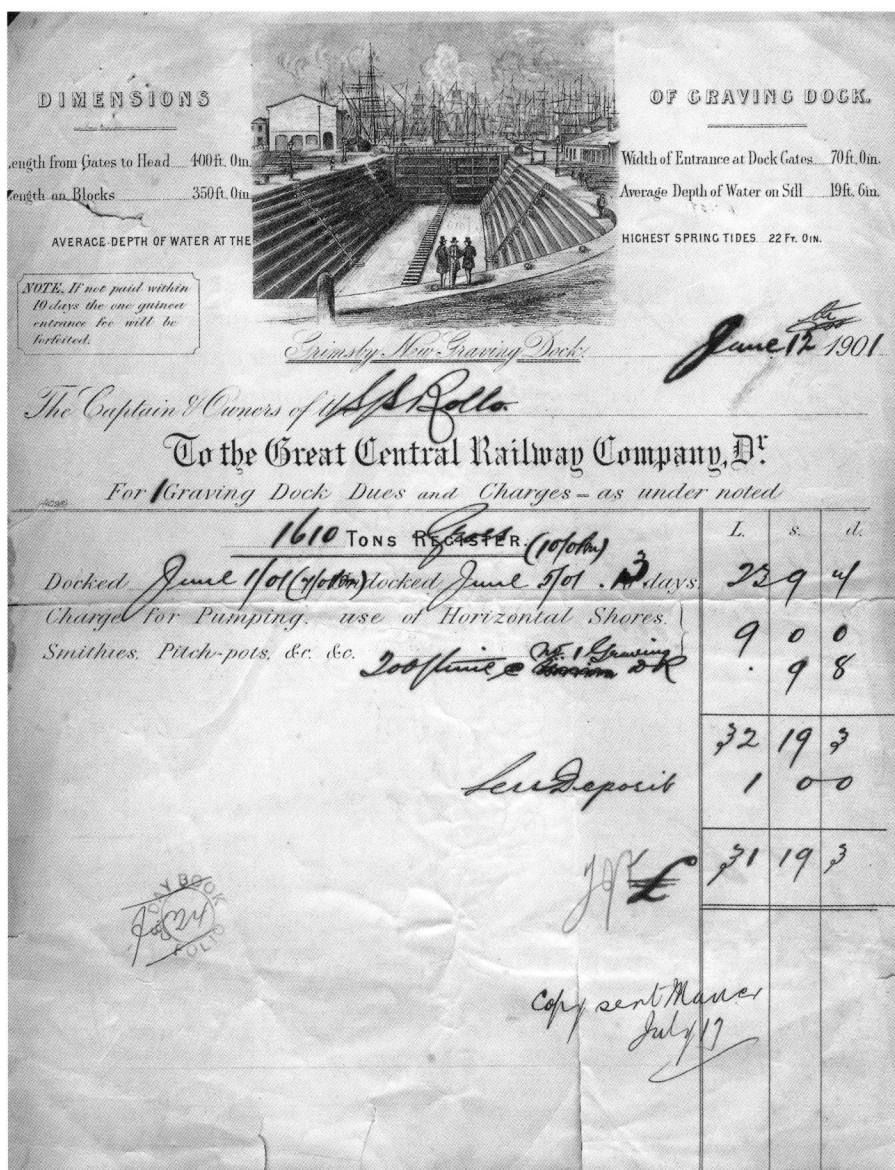

The Graving Dock was operated by the Railway Company who charged a daily rate based on the Gross Registered Tonnage (GRT) of the vessel. The S.S. 'Rollo' having a GRT of 1610 and remaining in the dry dock for three days was invoiced for £23 9s 7d (£23.48). A further £9 9s 8d (£9.48) was added for pumping out the water and refilling when the work was completed together with the provision of ancillary services including tool time. (ABP)

between. The piers varied in length from 40 to 80 feet (12.19 to 24.38 metres) and were generally six feet thick except towards the north end of the Dock where they were increased to 15 feet (4.57 metres) to provide foundations for the cranes. This method of construction was regarded as a little unusual at the time but according to present day engineers it would appear that this was adopted to overcome weight problems being experienced at the southern end of the Dock. The solid walls and quays initially built along

the first stages of the eastern embankment had placed severe pressure on the soft clay foreshore. To help prevent this problem re-occuring as work progressed further along the dock towards the lock, Rendell introduced the arches. It is possible, when the water in the Dock is at a sufficiently low level, to see the top of the arches today.

In addition to the main dock structures, Rendell also allowed for the provision of transit sheds, bonded warehouses and associated facilities. A railway station was constructed at the northern end of the Dock to allow passengers arriving/departing by train to embark/disembark as close as possible to the quayside. Tracks and turntables were laid to create a link with the main line of the railway, for the purpose of conveying goods direct to the cranes and warehouses adjacent to the quays.

The New Dock provided a whole range of facilities not previously available at Grimsby. The Port could now offer visiting vessels berths that were adjacent, not only to purpose-built covered storage areas, but also to rail transport that was able to convey goods quickly to and from any destination in the country. This whole new concept of handling seaborne trade in the Town had not, however, been without substantial financial commitment by the Railway Company. The MS&L had invested approximately £1,050,000 in the venture, of which £112,207

was attributable to the purchase of the Old Dock and outfall, with the remaining £937,793 being for the purchase of the land, together with reclamation and new construction works.

It is apparent, from reports written after the Dock was opened, that the work would not have been possible if it had not been for the efforts of John Rendell and his team. The main contractor Messrs. Hutching, Brown & Wright, together with Messrs. Lynn of Liverpool, who was engaged to build the cofferdam, also played an important part in the project. In addition, they were supported by other firms including Messrs. G. Forrester & Co. of Liverpool who provided ancillary equipment, such as a beam engine and boilers used in the six mortar mills erected next to the construction site.

An artist's impression of the Fish Dock showing the New Dock together with a pit in the background reportedly used to extract clay for the Dock Tower bricks, circa 1855.

CHAPTER SIX

The "Royal" Connection

By 27 March 1852 the Illustrated London News was reporting that the initial construction works were nearing completion. The Railway Company, in having the authority to reclaim an area of 135 acres (54.63 hectares) from the adjoining Humber, had already created an enclosed water area of more than 25 acres (10.12 hectares) with quays extending 3,600 feet (1,108.8 metres) in length.

To celebrate this great achievement, the contractors, Messrs. Hutchings, Brown and Wright, decided to mark the occasion by hosting a banquet. This was to take place on Thursday 18 March within the confines of the large lock-pit. The opportunities of using this structure to accommodate such an event were limited as the piles of the cofferdam were ready to be removed, thereby allowing water and shipping direct access to the Dock.

A marquee was erected in the 70 foot (21.56 metre) lock, big enough to cater for 300 people. Mr. Longhurst of the Yarborough Arms provided the entertainment, and special trains from London and Manchester were chartered to convey invitees to the event. Shipping in the Old Dock was decked in colourful bunting and the whole Dock Estate took part in the celebration. As the guests made their way down specially constructed stairs from the quay apron to the bottom of the lock, the Earl of Yarborough took the chair and soon after two o'clock the "Health of Her Majesty" was toasted to rapturous cheers.

Although this occasion provided an opportunity for the Railway Company and its contractors to mark the completion of the works it was mainly a private celebration. However, the Mayor considered that the whole Town should commemorate the construction of the New Dock. He issued the request that on Thursday 27 May 1852 when the Dock was

The banquet held in the large lock on 18 March 1852 to commemorate the completion of the work. It is known that this event took place in the large lock rather than the small lock because the illustration clearly shows both the flood and the ebb gates to the right of the tower. (Illustrated London News)

to open a general Holiday should be granted.

It was arranged that a procession should leave the Town Hall at one o'clock and proceed along the turnpike to the Dock. This was to be led by merchants and tradesmen of the Port, followed by representatives of the Benefit Societies who would be dressed in their official garments despatched from London especially for the occasion. Sunday School children were also encouraged to join the parade as it made its colourful way through the Town.

The event took place as planned and drew large numbers of visitors. There was a carnival atmosphere with bands, peels of church bells and flags fluttering in the breeze. When the procession arrived at the lock just before twelve noon the ceremony commenced. The tide was at its highest thereby enabling the first vessel, the tugboat 'Cumberland', to sail through the lock. She had the privilege of carrying Directors and Officials of the Railway Company and was greeted with Rule Britannia and cheers from the assembled crowds. She was followed by a Government cutter, then by the 'Columbine' from New Holland and the 'Pelham' from Hull. The first commercial vessel was the 'City of Norwich' which berthed adjacent to the newly constructed transit sheds on the East Side of the Dock where she started loading her cargo. By midnight, twelve hours after she had arrived, she left the Dock bound for Hamburg.

The celebrations had been a great success. It was estimated that in the region of six thousand had gathered along the quayside to witness the opening of the Dock. Hundreds had attended the huge tea party that had been arranged in the goods station for the poor and labouring classes. They had been accommodated at five tables measuring 150 feet (45.72 metres) in length and entertained by music and dancing. At six o'clock toys were given out at the Yarborough Hotel by Messrs. Hutching & Company, the contractors, and the days events concluded with fireworks at lock Hill provided by Mr. Scanman.

Although no members of the Royal Family

The trowel used by Albert Prince Consort to lay the foundation stone of the New Dock, 18 April 1849.
(Illustrated London News)

attended the opening ceremony in 1852, Prince Albert had laid the foundation stone during his visit to the town on Wednesday 18 April 1849.

He had travelled by train the previous day to Brocklesby Station where he was met by approximately 600 yeomen and farmers. Mounted on horseback they escorted the Prince as he travelled in a carriage to Brocklesby Hall, the home of the Earl of Yarborough. The following day he continued his journey by train to the construction area. His railway carriage, in which he was accompanied by the Earl and other officials, was pulled into the working area by 100 navvies, all dressed in white smock frocks, night-caps and blue favours. Greeted by groups of cheering on-lookers the carriage passed under a triumphal arch bearing the sign "Long live the Earl of Yarborough".

The foundation stone was located into a recess within the lock wall some 35 feet (10.67 metres) below the high water mark. Weighing 11 tons (11.18 tonnes), it contained examples of the coins of the realm for the period, ranging from a five pound piece to a fraction of a farthing. In recognising the importance of the event Mr. William Heaford Daubney, the Mayor, together with the Burgesses of the Borough, ensured that the Prince would not forget the reception he had been given during his visit to the Town.

The construction of the New Dock must have made an impression on the Prince, for in 1854 he joined his wife, Queen Victoria, in making a second visit to the Port. This, however, was rather unexpected as it was only a few days prior to the visit that the Queen's intentions were conveyed to the Mayor, Dr. Robert Keetley.

The Royal family were staying at Balmoral and it was decided that as they returned south they would visit Grimsby. The letter to Dr. Keetley indicated that the Royal party would arrive at Hull during the evening of Friday 13 October. The following morning at 11 o'clock precisely Her Majesty would set sail from Hull on board the Royal Yacht

The Royal Yacht entering the large lock from the Royal Dock Basin during the visit of Queen Victoria and Prince Albert, 13 October 1854. (Illustrated London News)

'The Fairy' for Grimsby. The visit was not expected to be lengthy as the communiqué stated that she would proceed at 2 o'clock the same afternoon by train to London.

The short notice of their visit resulted in the Mayor, his fellow Council colleagues and the Dock owners embarking upon the rapid formulation of plans for the event. They were assisted by the Earl of Yarborough who immediately travelled to Balmoral in his dual capacity of Steward of the Borough and Chairman of the Railway Company, in order to discuss the arrangements of the Queen's reception with Sir George Grey.

Whilst the Earl of Yarborough was in Scotland efforts were being made to find a reception room large enough to cater for 1000 people. It was agreed that improvisation would have to be used in the form of the passenger station on the West Side of the Dock. A professional decorator was sent from Manchester to supervise the furnishing of the rooms. The main reception area was abundantly decorated with flags, Royal emblems and bunting in red, white and blue. The main feature of the furnishings was an attractive raised platform, over which was draped a rich velvet canopy in Royal purple.

The Royal Yacht arrived in the Dock Basin at approx 12.30 and sailed into the larger of the two lock-pits where Her Majesty, accompanied by her entourage, disembarked. They were received by the Earl of Yarborough, and escorted to the reception hall. The time allocated for the visit was short and therefore the ceremonial proceedings were brief. This did not, however, prevent the Directors of the Railway Company including a request within

*Shipping in the Royal Dock including the DFDS vessel the S.S. 'Olga' which was employed on the Denmark -
Newcastle/Leigh/Grimsby service from 1914 to 1919. (Chris Turner)*

Vessels being penned in the small lock. (Chris Turner)

The S.S. 'Margrethe' berthed at No. 7 quay ready to load coal via the adjacent coal drop. The other two vessels to her right are laying alongside the Coaling Jetty, which was removed in the late 1920's/early 1930's. (NELC Local Studies Library.)

their address to the Queen. They asked whether she would "graciously permit them to commemorate this auspicious and most gracious visit to our New Dock by granting permission to designate it in future as the Royal Dock". The request was subsequently granted thereby permitting the Dock to be known by that name thereafter.

The purpose of the visit could have originated from the curiosity of the Prince Consort to see the completion of the works, for which he had laid the foundation stone five years earlier. The Queen, who always appeared to be interested in her husband's projects, agreed to break their journey south in order to fulfil his wishes.

The visit also benefited the Town in that it provided an opportunity for the Corporation to commemorate the occasion by renaming the whole length of Victoria Street in honour of Her Majesty. It had previously been called by three different names, depending upon the section to which you were referring. The first stretch from the Black Swan at the junction of

Flottergate was named Baxtergate West. This was followed by North Saint Mary's Gate, which formed the remaining part of the square with the present East, West and South Saint Mary's Gate. These four roads surrounded Grimsby's original parish church of Saint Mary that was reputed to have had a tower rivalling that of Boston Stump. Moving on from North Saint Mary's Gate the road returned to Baxtergate, but on this occasion being distinguished from its predecessor by the suffix of East. This section terminated at the junction with George Street from where it was then called Loft Street, after Major General John Henry Loft who had been elected Member of Parliament for Grimsby in 1802.

Victoria Street continued to form part of the turnpike that travelled south to Wold Newton. It was also the main thoroughfare from which the Town dwellers could gain access to the Old Dock by means of the three staiths, as required by the Grimsby Haven Act.

The Royal Dock showing a sailing vessel moored against the western Coaling Jetty. The Jetty in the background was originally constructed to allow timber to be lifted directly from the dock and loaded into railway wagons. It was later converted for the handling of vessels loading coal. (Chris Turner)

The Dock Offices, completed in the autumn of 1885, were constructed to provide a new administrative centre for the Port Authority at Grimsby. The original Dock Offices were located on the East Side of the Royal Dock and were shared by the Railway Company and John Sutcliffe & Son. Following the opening of the new building, its predecessor was leased directly to Sutcliffe's as their main office. (ABP)

The transit sheds on the West Side of the Royal Dock provide extensive covered accommodation for goods awaiting shipment. (NELC Welholme Galleries)

Above The four rail tracks provide a direct means of conveying goods to and from the adjoining transit sheds. A system was installed whereby wagons travelling along the line on the left of the photograph could be turned at right angles and moved into the sheds. This was achieved by placing the wagons on turntables and using horses to manoeuvre them into the adjoining covered accommodation. (NELC Welholme Galleries)

Turntables for manoeuvring the rail wagons in and out of the East Side sheds were also located adjacent to the quays. Work appears to be underway to either remove or renew the existing track. (ABP)

CHAPTER SEVEN

The Dock Tower

The construction of the New Dock undoubtedly resulted in an increase in trade for Grimsby. However, it also provided a unique structure that has, for 150 years, been a prominent symbol of the Port together with the adjoining Town. Standing like an isolated beacon to greet mariners to the Humber, the Dock Tower has become a landmark and a significant example of local Victorian engineering.

Soaring 309 feet (94.18 metres) to the top of the lantern, the Tower is regarded as a fine specimen of plain brickwork, the material for which had been extracted from the marsh adjoining the Dock. Completed on 27 March 1852 its style is of a rectangular design, measuring 28 feet square (2.60 square metres) at the base and tapering to 26 feet (7.92 metres) to the underside of the first projections. The walls vary in thickness from four feet (1.21 metres) at its foundation to three feet (0.91 metres) at the string course under the corbels and are estimated to contain a total of one million bricks.

A wrought iron tank capable of storing 33,000 gallons (7,260 litres) of water was positioned within the larger of the projecting balconies at a height of approximately 200 feet (60.96 metres) from the ground. Water was forced into the tank by the use of two force pumps each measuring 10 inches (25.4 centimetres) in diameter. These, in turn, were worked by a duplicate 25 horse powered horizontal engine located at the Dock entrance. The water, which was sourced from a well 15 feet (4.57 metres) in diameter and 47 feet (14.33 metres) deep, was then transported through a 13 inch (33.02 centimetre) diameter cast iron pipe along the East Side of the Dock, across both the Graving Dock and 45 feet (14.63 metres) lock

before entering the base of the Tower. The pipework within the building was located adjacent to the east wall and can still be seen today. All the pumps, engines and associated pipes were manufactured by Mr. Mitchell at

The Dock Tower, a grade one listed building, symbolises the achievement of local Victorian engineering. (Chris Turner)

his Perran Foundry in Cornwall.

This method of providing pressurised water for the operation of hydraulic appliances had been designed by Sir William George Armstrong. Originally a lawyer by profession he turned his attention to the use of hydraulics in engineering. One of his first successful applications was achieved in 1846, when he powered a crane by water obtained from the mains supply in Newcastle. He went on to develop his system, opening a factory at Elswick on the banks of the Tyne, from where he also manufactured breach loader guns and iron ships.

During the development stages of his hydraulic research Armstrong found that, when using the town mains to power his appliances, fluctuations would occur thereby creating uneven levels of pressure. To overcome this problem at Grimsby he decided that the fifteen quayside cranes, lock gates and sluices should be provided with an alternative supply of water.

In order to achieve this objective, Armstrong came to the conclusion that a tank should be placed high above the ground with a direct feed into the machinery. To accommodate his requirements Mr. James William Wild designed the Dock Tower on the style of the Palazzo Publico in Siena, Italy, which is similar to the Tower of Birmingham University. Originally intended to serve as a hydraulic tower and lighthouse, it has only been used in the former capacity. It was found that to locate a light at such a height would result in it being seen from a great distance in the North Sea. Although this would have had certain advantages, it was considered that mariners could have confused it with the Spurn lights.

Whilst the Dock Tower was under construction Armstrong was in the process of developing an alternative system using accumulators. He had found that a greater hydraulic pressure could be achieved by employing more compact and less expensive machinery. In recognising the advantages of his new design, he installed the first system at New Holland Dock Pier. Although this event took place more than a year prior to Grimsby's hydraulic scheme being commissioned, work continued with the building of the Dock Tower.

Unfortunately the use of hydraulic pressure from this source was eventually replaced. A hydraulic accumulator tower was constructed on the opposite side of the lock some 70 yards (64 metres) to the North West of the Dock Tower. This became operational in 1892 and although the Dock and lock machinery are now powered by electric or electro-hydraulic energy, the accumulator tower still remains and has been designated as a grade two star listed building.

For many years following the construction of the Dock Tower, a myth existed suggesting the foundations were built on cotton wool. This raised much interest and even as late as 1964 a letter, from Mr. E. Maple of London, was received by the Port Master seeking further information in order to clarify the rumours he had heard. It was explained that it was a common Lincolnshire belief that high structures including Boston Stump were constructed on cotton wool or other similar material. The origins of the fallacy appeared to stem from the fact that early in the Nineteenth Century, Lincolnshire had a large sheep industry and the wool from the famous Lincoln Long Wool Sheep was exported through the Port. It could therefore have been construed that the new Dock and its facilities were built from the dock dues and wharfage revenue accruing from possibly, at that time, the Port's main trade.

In April 1961 a reporter, employed by the Grimsby Evening Telegraph, traced a gentleman in New Holland whose father helped construct the Dock Tower. He stated that it was built on faggots or bundles of boards. However, according to the plans accompanying the report presented to the Institution of Civil Engineers by Edward Hele Clark on 29 November 1864, there appears little to suggest that anything other than wooden piles were used in supporting the foundations of the Dock Tower.

One interesting feature of the Tower, which unfortunately does not exist today, was its hydraulic lift. Although it is not recorded as being installed at the time of construction, it is reported that Queen Victoria gave permission for Prince Albert, the Prince of Wales and the Princess Royal to use it when visiting the gallery above the water tank on 14 October 1854. It appears that the lift remained in regular operation until the outbreak of the Second World War. During the 1930's many people ascended the Tower and were charged sixpence for the privilege. It is

assumed, as a result of the numbers involved, that they used the lift rather than climbing the 445 steps, as they would do today.

Although this piece of apparatus was generally employed for the conveyance of individuals to the viewing area, it also had its less pleasant uses as reported by the Grimsby Telegraph on 10 September 1923. On this occasion James Davis, a foreman steeplejack from Manchester, was placing the last plank of wood in position on scaffolding when he had a seizure and died. He had been accompanying Mr. Tarrant, the Assistant Docks Engineer, around the three storey staging that had been erected ready to carry out maintenance work. Whilst climbing over the parapet to regain access to the balcony of the Tower he experienced his attack and fell backwards into the arms of Mr. Tarrant. Mr. Davis's son, who had been assisting in the work, witnessed the incident and escorted his father's body as it was lowered in the lift and

The three storey scaffolding around the Dock Tower provides a clear indication of the risks undertaken by Mr. Davis as a steeplejack. (Chris Turner)

taken to hospital to await an inquest.

The Tower has provided Grimsby with a unique historic monument, which is now nationally recognised having being given a grade one listing by English Heritage. It ranks with some of the most prestigious buildings in the country including Buckingham Palace. It would, however, be interesting to consider the outcome if Armstrong had realised earlier the benefits of using smaller accumulator towers to achieve the same hydraulic power. If this had been the case, it is extremely unlikely the Town would have such an outstanding landmark today.

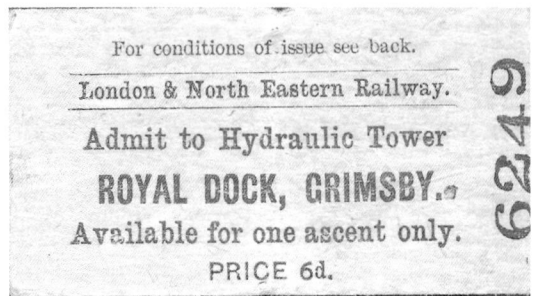

A ticket costing 6d (2¹/₂ pence) to ascend the Dock Tower by the lift, issued by the London and North Eastern Railway Company. (ABP)

An extract from the Dock Master's cash book recording the number of tickets issued to the public during 16 & 17 August 1939. (ABP)

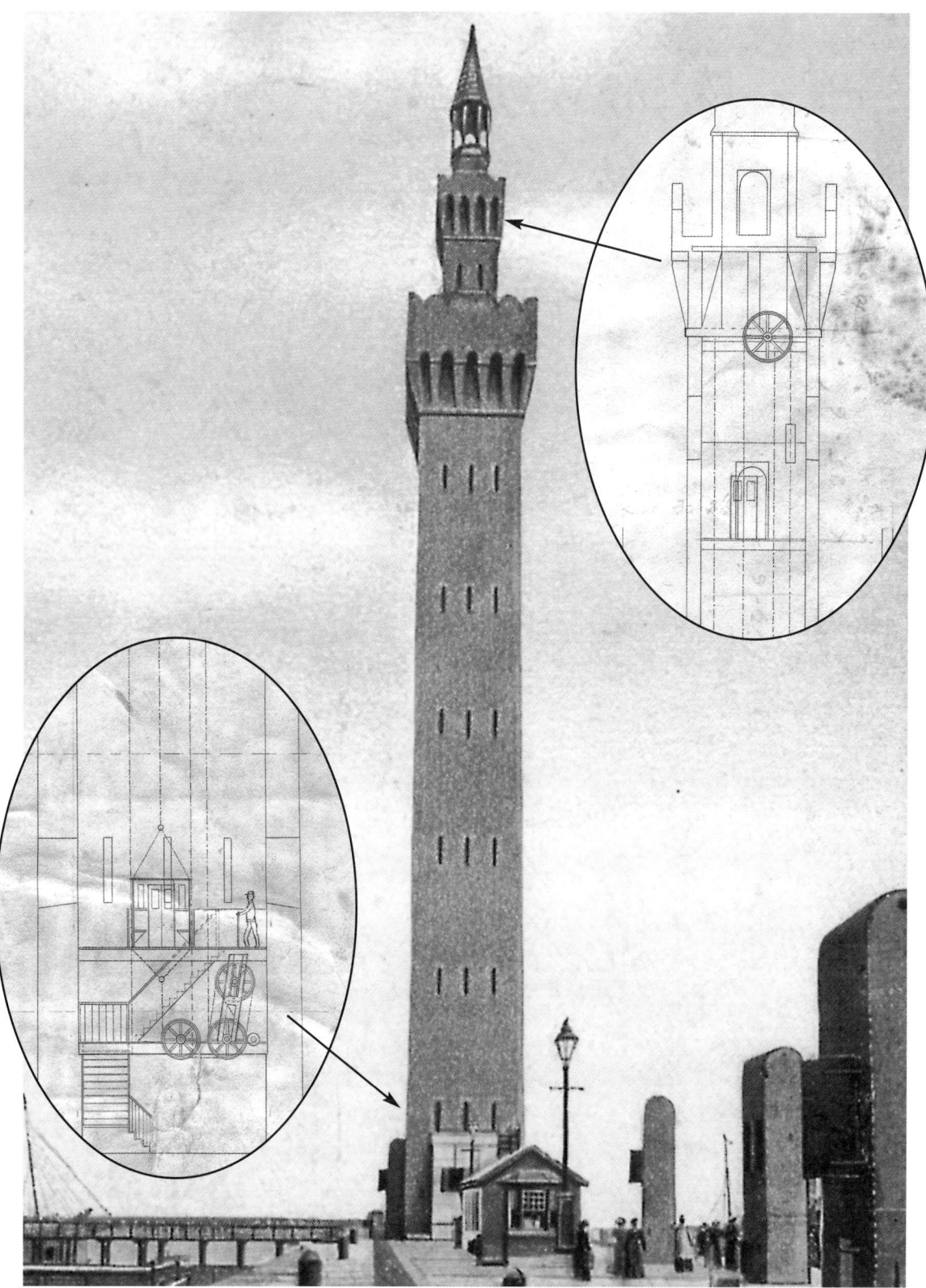

The Dock Tower showing the location of the lift mechanism. (ABP)

CHAPTER EIGHT

The Development of Trade and the Need for Expansion

As the New Dock neared completion the MS&L started a campaign to market its new facilities. It published a booklet entitled "Description of the New Docks at Great Grimsby with map and plan".

This was the first step of attracting additional trade to the Port.

One of the main problems the Railway Company had to overcome related to the location of the Town. At that time, Grimsby

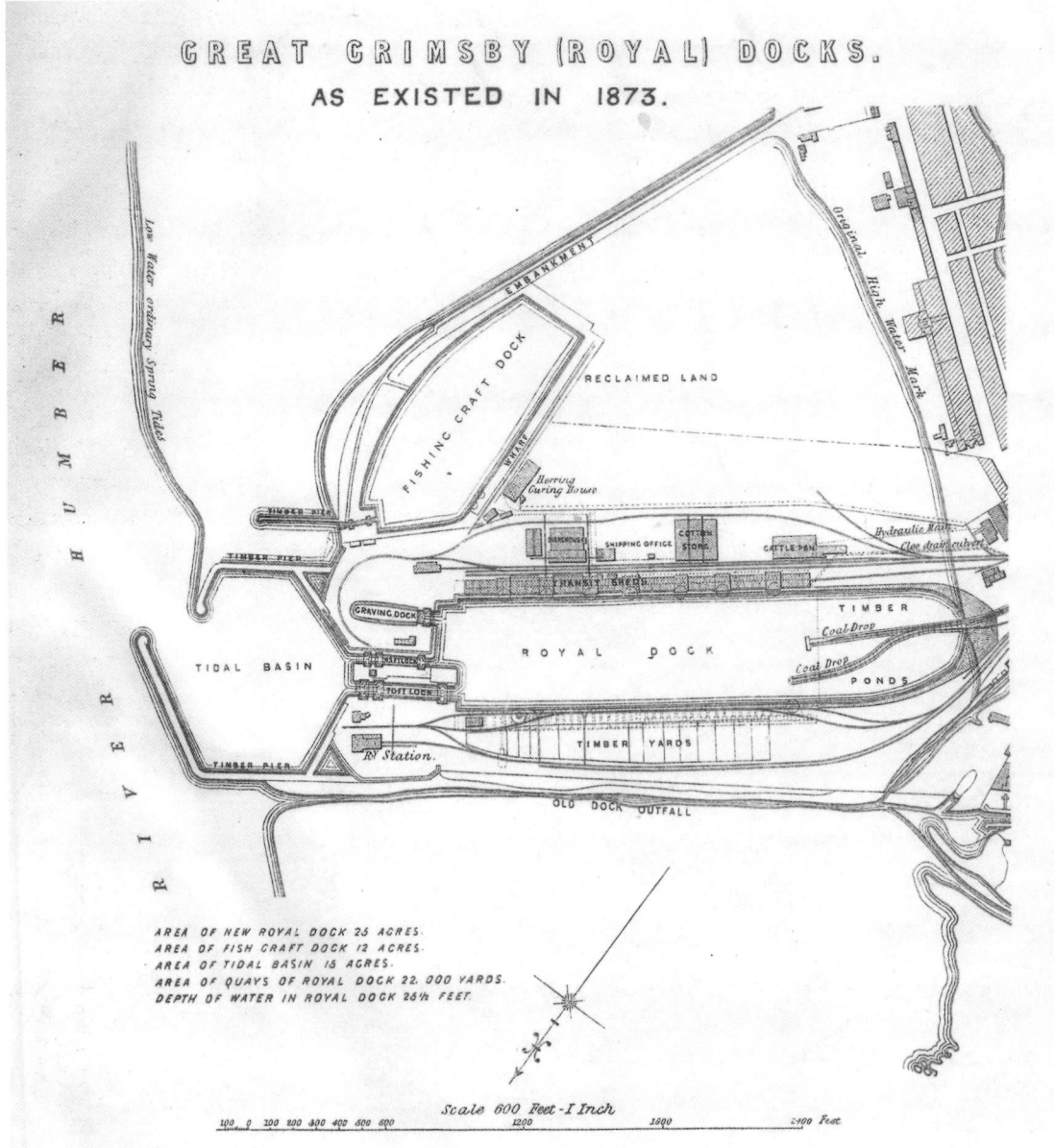

1873 Plan of the Royal Dock. (Cosalt)

was a relatively small County Borough with a population, in 1851, of 8,638. Until the coming of the railways in 1848 the Port was unable to offer any substantial means of transporting goods to or from its quays. Its reputation, therefore, did not have a great deal to be desired. The Railway Company had rather an uphill struggle, but it was already attempting to promote the benefits it was able to provide.

The landward communication links were well established by the time the Dock opened in 1852. They could provide a direct means of transporting cargoes to or from any destination on the mainland within hours. The Dock was able to offer a water area in excess of 25 acres (16.12 hectares) including a timber pond at the southern end. It could also boast that it would never contain less than 25 feet (7.62 metres) at the north end, gradually reducing to 20 feet (6.10 metres) at the timber pond. Its capabilities of accommodating a whole fleet of war steam-ships, should the need arise, assisted in demonstrating the size of the facilities available. In addition, it also illustrated the closeness of the Port to the German Ocean, which was estimated to be only half-an-hour's steaming time away.

Timber had, for many years, been a prime commodity handled at Grimsby, but with the availability of an additional 5 acres (2.02 hectares) of ponds the potential existed to increase the tonnage passing through the Port. This prospect was not overlooked and by 1865 181,352 tons (184,254 tonnes) had been imported, a rise of 134% compared with 1860. Perhaps the provision of two rail lines, mounted on piles, and extending out through the ponds, had assisted in achieving this increase. The travelling cranes also on the jetty could remove the timber at one lift from the water and place it directly into rail wagons.

Timber was not the only traffic increasing in volume as a result of the new facilities. Coal had been a significant trade passing through the Port for some years, but by 1864, 155,205 tons (157,698 tonnes) had been handled, the quantity having almost quadrupled in ten years. Although this upturn in business was now gathering momentum there had been initial concerns that regular shipping services were not being attracted to the New Dock. Fortunately the Railway Company addressed this problem by forming an arrangement with the North of Europe Steamship Company to provide a weekly passenger and cargo service to Hamburg. This new link with the Continent commenced twelve hours after the 'City of Norwich' had arrived in Grimsby as the first commercial vessel to pass through the new lock.

One of the earliest photographs of the Royal Dock showing the timber pond in the foreground. circa 1856 (NELC Local Studies Library)

The line proved extremely popular and it soon introduced a weekly schedule to Rotterdam. By 1854 the demand was so great that it had to double its sailings to Hamburg. This prosperity, however, did not continue and the subsequent formation of the Anglo French Steamship Company placed great pressure on the North of Europe Steamship Company to compete for traffic. The Company was beginning to find it difficult to operate but continued to trade with the Port until September 1856 when it eventually withdrew its ships. As it struggled against competing lines operating out of Hull, Newcastle and West Hartlepool it saw its fleet slowly diminish. A number of vessels were lost through accidents whilst others were removed from service as a result of the depressing state of commerce at that time. By 1860 serious consideration was given to the liquidation of the Company. Although this was resisted it forced a closer examination of the way in which Anglo French operated.

The MS&L had promoted the formation of Anglo French in order to transport coal from South Yorkshire to France. However, the original intention of the Railway Company was to amend its articles of association in order to include the chartering of vessels as part of its business. When this was refused it decided to support an independent line and issued a prospectus detailing the economic reasons for the creation of the new Company. As a result of this, Anglo French was formed on 13 March 1856 under the Chairmanship of Lord Yarborough. The MS&L, as the prime advocate of the venture, became the largest shareholder in association with the South Yorkshire Railway, the River Don Company and a number of French coal importers.

The shipping line was able to handle its first traffic when it took delivery of its maiden vessel the S.S. 'Eugenie' in April 1856. A further eight iron steamships were on order from Messrs. Samuelson of Hull, and in July of the same year the S.S. 'Victoria' together with the S.S. 'Napoleon' arrived in Grimsby ready to carry coal to Dieppe, Rouen, Bordeaux and Le Havre. Two additional vessels joined the fleet later in the year, which

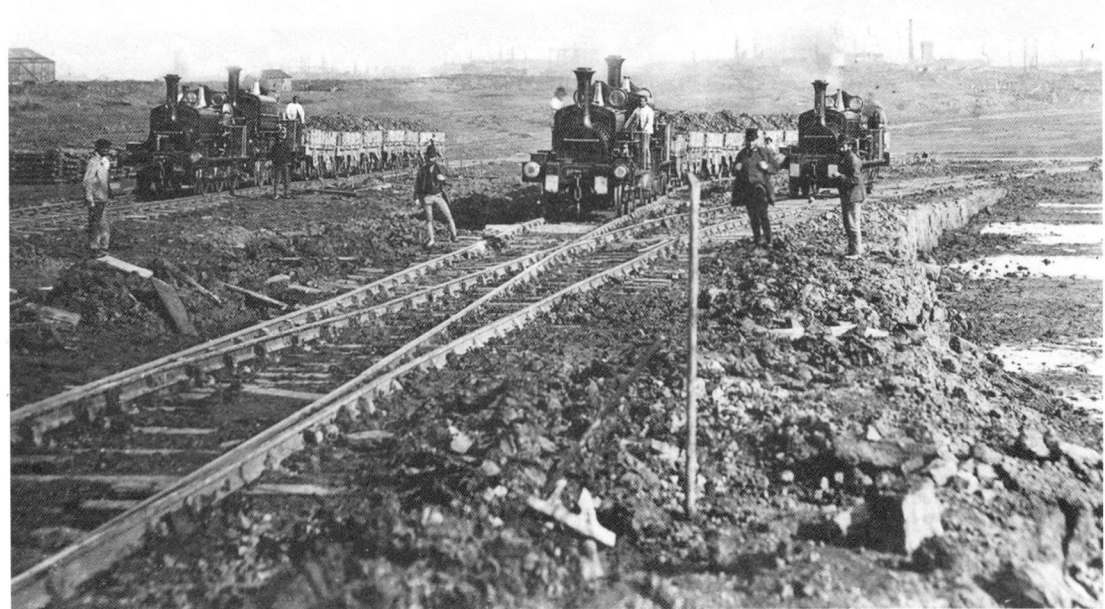

Messrs. Logan & Hemmingway, contractors for the expansion of the Old Dock, engaged in the removal of the earth from the construction site circa mid 1870's. (NELC Local Studies Library)

enabled the Company to transport over 46,000 tons (46,736 tonnes) during its first year of operation. The remaining four ships were commissioned in 1857, thereby permitting the Company to extend its service to Hamburg, Stettin and Cronstadt.

With the assistance of Anglo French the trade passing through the Port continued to increase. By 1865 Grimsby had become the fifth port in the Kingdom with the value of its export traffic alone exceeding six and a half million pounds per annum. Unfortunately this resulted in adverse consequences in that the berthing capacity available could not meet the escalating demand. In acknowledging the problem the Railway Company accepted a proposal by Messrs. Logan & Hemmingway to construct a 26-acre (10.52 hectares) dock adjoining the Old Dock. This was located at right angles to the existing water space on land that had partly been used for open storage. It was also decided to progress with the construction of a link between the Old Dock and the Royal Dock thereby preventing

vessels from having to pass through the two separate entrance locks in order to move from one dock to the other.

Both projects commenced in 1872 and took seven years to complete. The link, which became the Union Dock (also referred to as the Cutting), was opened on 22 July 1879 by Their Royal Highnesses the Prince and Princess of Wales, who later became King Edward VII and Queen Alexandra. During their visit they also unveiled a statue of Prince Albert that had been erected by Sir Edward Watkin, M.P. in the gardens opposite the Royal Hotel.

In recognition of the Royal visit the new West Arm together with the Old Dock were renamed Alexandra Dock in honour of the Princess of Wales. The total water area to the south of the original lock entrance now amounted to 49 acres (19.83 hectares) which made Alexandra Dock one of the largest docks in existence at that time. Costing £55,367 to complete, it was able to provide specially adapted quays for the handling of timber, a

The Royal Party proceeding through the Union Dock into the Royal Dock on board the Company's Steamer 'Manchester'. 22 July, 1879. (Illustrated London News)

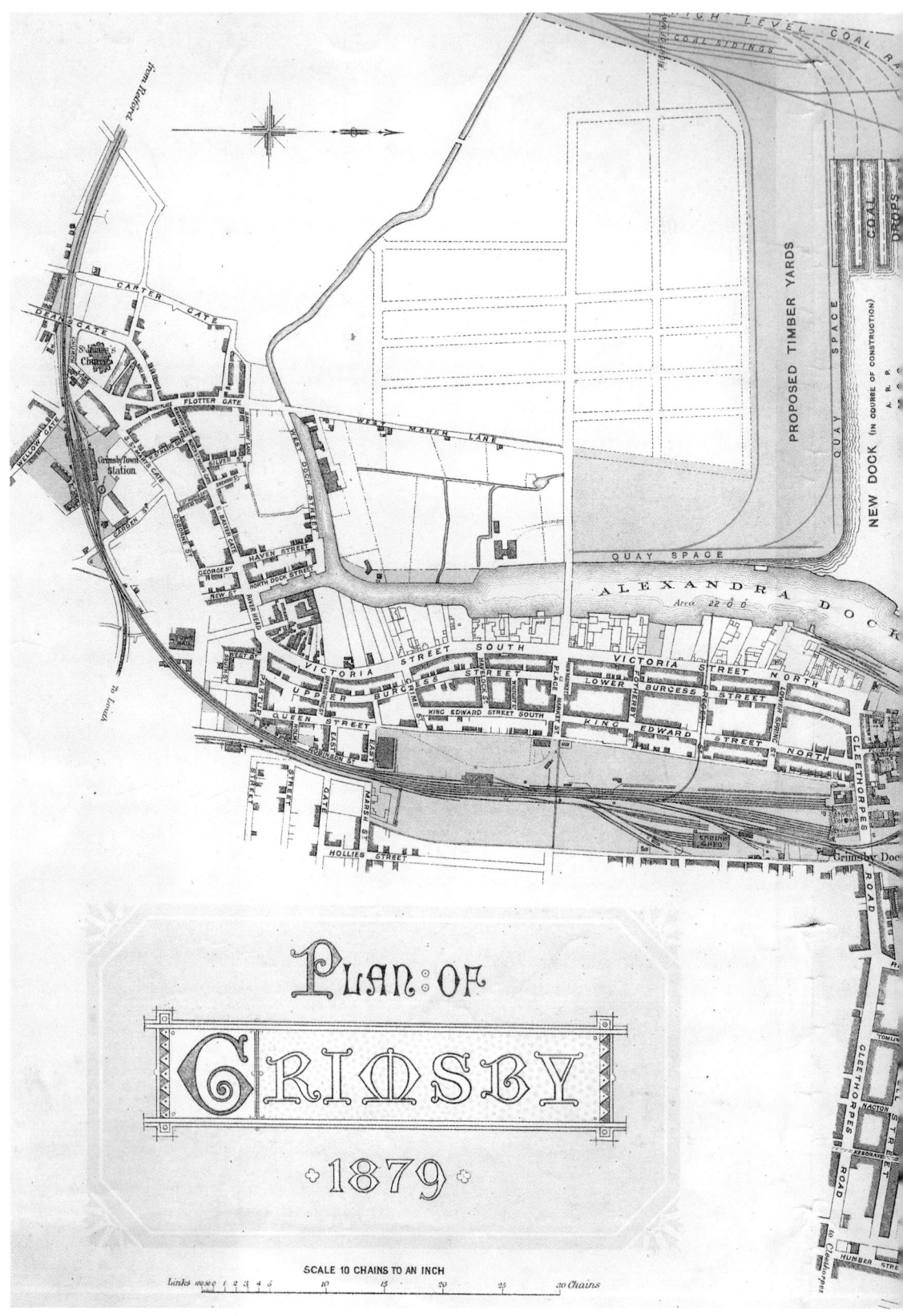

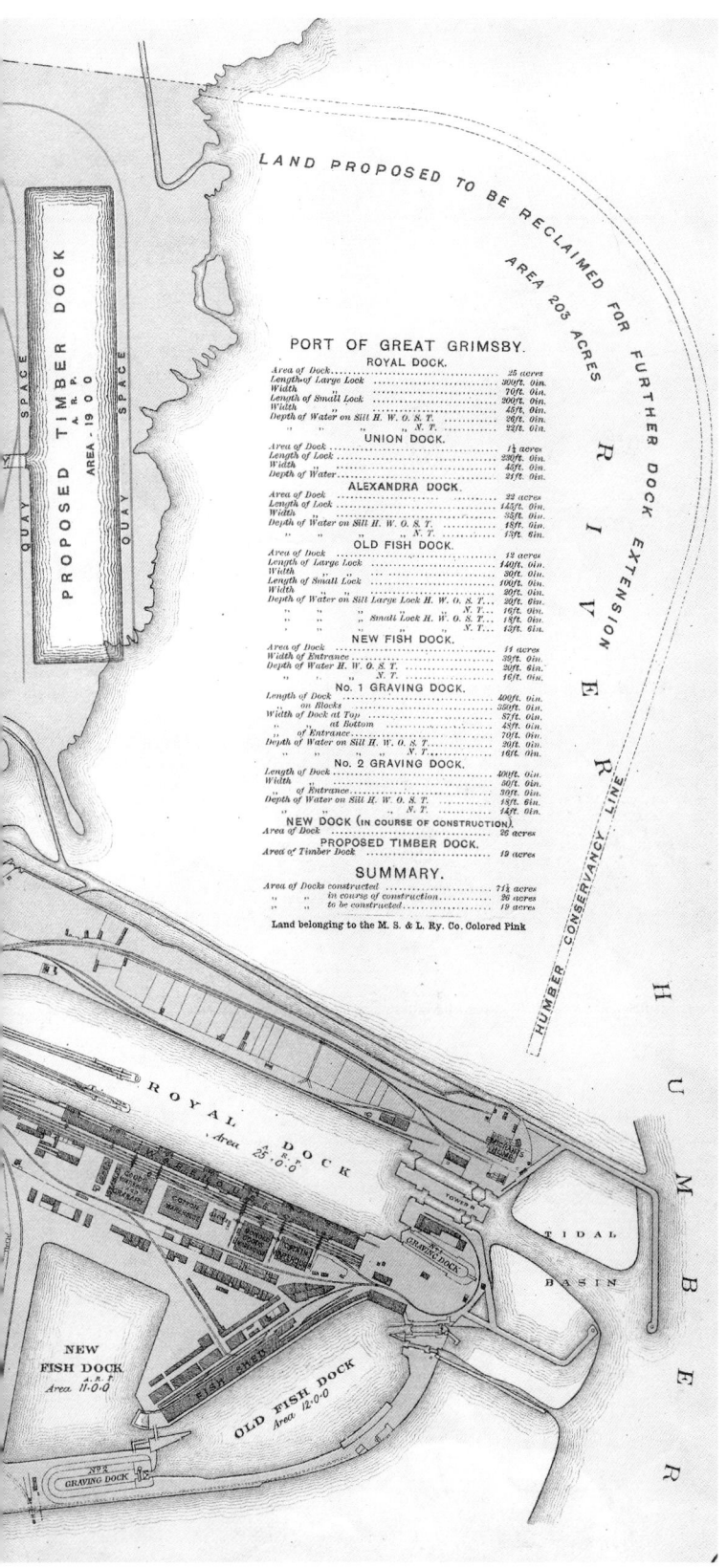

1879 plan of Grimsby Docks showing the area under construction that was later to become the West Arm of Alexandra Dock. The proposed timber pond never progressed and now forms part of the Volkswagen Terminal. (ABP)

become its main trade. During the following years Grimsby was to experience a substantial rise in timber traffic and by 1911 approximately 400,000 tons (406,400 tonnes) per annum was passing through Alexandra Dock. The loading of coal could also be accommodated within the new West Arm. Two purpose-built parallel jetties had been constructed at the western end of the Dock upon which was erected two coal drops. These were served by rail wagons from West Marsh Junction that would be shunted and pushed up the two earth embankments onto the jetties. Whilst the embankments remained until the 1960's the jetties had been removed by the 1950's.

The unveiling of a bronze statue of Albert Prince Consort by Their Royal Highnesses the Prince and Princess of Wales to mark their visit to Grimsby. (Illustrated London News)

Prince Albert statue was originally located in the gardens opposite the Royal Hotel. This building was designed by M. E. Hadfield & Son of Sheffield and constructed by John Brown of Grimsby. Originally known as the Royal Dock Hotel it opened in 1865 at a cost of £5000 and was demolished in 1966 before the erection of the Cleethorpe Road flyover. (NELC Welholme Galleries)

CHAPTER NINE

One Hundred and Forty Years Service to the Port

Although the MS&L had been directly responsible for attracting substantial trade through the Port, other individuals and organisations had also played their part. Perhaps the most notable was a gentleman, originally from Rochdale, who moved to Grimsby in 1862 to take up an appointment with Anglo French.

John Sutcliffe started his career in the offices of a small merchant within the expanding Port of Liverpool. Although his duties are not known it is thought he would have been involved with some part of the shipping industry. Perhaps as a result of the contacts he formed with possible agents, carriers or warehousemen, he was able to secure his second appointment with the Carvex Company. This business helped to arrange for the carriage, storage and shipment of goods imported and exported by its clients, which, no doubt, provided the new employee with invaluable experience. He continued to progress well with the Company and was highly regarded by his peers.

In the late 1840's, however, he was offered a position with the newly incorporated Lancashire & Yorkshire Railway Company that demanded greater responsibility. He initially moved to Brighouse where he became Goods Agent but by 22 December 1848 he had been appointed to the position of Townsman in Manchester. By 1851 his success in developing a sound knowledge of the Company's operation was rewarded by a promotion to Huddersfield as Goods Agent in the Traffic Department. Two years later he moved again, this time taking up a post in Bradford. Unfortunately this was to be his last move with the Company. He had realised that the ability for further advancement was losing momentum and subsequently accepted an approach from representatives of the North British Railway.

The working relationship with his new employer did not appear to last very long, as later in 1857 he had been recruited by the West Hartlepool Steam Navigation Company as Shipping Agent. It was during the five years, whilst in the North East of England, that he gained the necessary experience required to fulfil the needs of the work he was later to undertake in Grimsby.

In 1862 he moved for the final time and

Insert, John Sutcliffe, founder of the Company. (John Sutcliffe & Son (Grimsby) Limited)

settled in Stallingborough, where he took up residence in the Manor House. At the age of 49 his career was entering a new phase, which was to result in the formation of John Sutcliffe & Company on 30 June of the same year. Located in the Royal Dock Chambers, the business was solely concerned with the provision of a shipping and forwarding agency for the Anglo French Steamship Company. This facility was funded through a 5% return received on all freight passing over the Grimsby to Hamburg route. As time progressed the firm diversified and became general commission agents and shipbrokers, thereby extending its client base. However, its principal activity remained with Anglo French until it ceased trading in 1865.

Although the Port was experiencing buoyant times, there were frequent fluctuations in the volume of trade passing over the quays. In addition Grimsby was often confronted with intense competition from Goole, Hull and West Hartlepool. This did not assist John Sutcliffe in securing traffic for Anglo French and its Hamburg service. Fortunately, whilst employed in West Hartlepool, he had gained a sound knowledge of the individuals who were now creating a "price war" within the shipping industry. In order to try and regain market share he decided to approach the problem using the same tactics as his competitors. He visited the Company's Agent in Hamburg, Mr. H. C. Rover, a person with whom he had formed a strong relationship some years earlier. The men agreed that a reduction of 10% in existing charges was required. Although this was to prove an expensive solution to the problem it was supported by the Directors and within two months Anglo French had re-established its position in the market.

Unfortunately this was not the end of the

A selection of vessels in the Royal Dock likely to have been handled by John Sutcliffe & Son. (ABP)

matter. The West Hartlepool group would not enter into negotiations and subsequently reduced their rates further in respect of worsted yarns and manufactures. They then suggested that each port should concentrate its efforts on generating trade within its own locality. This proposal would have placed Grimsby and Hull at a great disadvantage and was therefore entirely unacceptable. It was during a period of relative calm, when the market share between the three ports remained unchanged, that John Sutcliffe started to promote the service that could be offered. He adopted a policy specifically designed to improve the efficiency of the business that he and his principals could provide to the customer. His efforts assisted in restarting negotiations with representatives from West Hartlepool who eventually acknowledged that their actions had been the cause of the disruption.

Despite John Sutcliffe's actions to resolve the problems and develop trade, Anglo French was finally dissolved in 1865. A reduction in traffic partially caused by the impact of the American Civil War (1861-65) had resulted in the Directors losing confidence in the business. They had, for some time, been reluctant to invest in new vessels and the fleet was now ageing and underpowered. John Sutcliffe however, was aware that changes were inevitable and started to consider the alternatives that may be on the horizon.

The Directors of the Railway Company were also considering their future direction. They had already expressed their intentions to expand their overseas business. It was with this objective in mind that they examined the possibility of entering negotiations with a consortium led by John Lumsden of Hull. The Directors were of the opinion that an independent shipping firm could provide a comparable service rather than invest in their own fleet. John Sutcliffe was not particularly

pleased with this thought as he could see potential competition and therefore decided to intervene. He presented a case with such skill that it changed the future of Grimsby together with the fortunes of his own business.

In April 1866, John Sutcliffe & Company signed a contract with the MS&L appointing them sole Agents for their fleet of vessels, thereby forming an association that was to last into the 20th Century. During that time Jack Sutcliffe, the son of John, had joined the Company and by 1872, at the age of twenty-seven, was made a full partner. In recognition of this event the firm changed its name to John Sutcliffe & Son.

The leadership of the firm passed to Jack following the death of his father on 24 December 1877. He continued to maintain the close relationship with the Railway Company that had been established over the years. However, he also started to take an interest in the activities of Thomas Wilson, Son & Company. It took many years of negotiation before he eventually persuaded the Company to operate a weekly line from Grimsby to Copenhagen and Malmo. This success was followed, twelve months later, by the appointment as Agents for the United Steamship Company of Copenhagen, which commenced operation on 16 June 1890.

Jack Sutcliffe made every effort to consolidate the activities of the business and build upon the foundations created by his father. His positive attitude assisted in the continued development of the Port. Grimsby had to compete for traffic with many other ports, and in doing so Jack's determination proved to be a great asset in attracting additional trade over the quays. During his term of office as head of the firm, he demonstrated an ability to make shrewd decisions, resulting in his involvement in the handling of many developing cargoes through the Port. This was not only to benefit his firm but also the Commercial Docks as a whole.

The death of Jack Sutcliffe saw the appointment of his son, Ernest, as the senior partner. He was supported by his uncle, Tom Sutcliffe who had decided to take a less dominant role in the firm following his brother's death. Their close working relationship was to last until 1931 when Tom died. Ernest was then left to continue his quest to secure whatever trade was available for Grimsby. This was not always easy and by 1936 it was decided to change the structure of the business.

John Sutcliffe & Son had always operated as a partnership and the firm's activities had been arranged as a single entity. However, as a result of changing economic conditions, action was taken to create two new Companies, each having its own separate area of responsibility. John Sutcliffe & Son (Grimsby) Limited was formed to co-ordinate the activities at the Port where it acted as master stevedores; handled coal, timber, bulk

and general cargoes; offered services including ship-broking, chartering, forwarding, customs clearance, agency, insurance; and provided warehousing and transport facilities. Its sister company John Sutcliffe & Son (Agencies) Limited was established to continue the business originally performed by the parent firm in the provinces. This involved controlling the work of the branch offices at Birmingham, Bradford, Liverpool and Manchester whose principal task was to secure cargoes and liaise between the shippers and the Ports of Grimsby and Immingham.

The financial returns achieved by John Sutcliffe & Son (Grimsby) Limited were regarded as being extremely satisfactory. Although the agency work for the railway vessels had been lost, the Company had retained a close involvement with the United Steamship Company of Copenhagen. Its long-term future was further assisted in 1947 when it was appointed agents and stevedores

Mourners attending the funeral of Alderman Jack Sutcliffe walk along Bethleham Street. (Garry Crossland)

for a new weekly service to the North and West Coasts of Norway operated by Nordenfjeldske Dampskibsselskab (NFDS).

John Sutcliffe & Son continued to develop over the years, creating other associated companies including John Sutcliffe Consolidated Stevedores. As the name implies this managed the stevedoring operations and was formed as a result of the decasualisation of labour under the Dock Labour Scheme in 1967. It incorporated the stevedoring activities of John Sutcliffe & Son (Grimsby)

Limited, East Coast River Services Limited, Moffat & Craigie Limited, Moffat & Trought Limited, Jacob Pickwell Limited and Arthur Smith.

By 1984 the Sutcliffe Group had decided to restructure its business and formed John Sutcliffe & Son (Holdings) Limited, to undertake the corporate administration and accounting for the whole of its operation. Although now located off the Dock Estate the influence of this Company remains extremely strong within the Port, and will no doubt continue to do so for many years to come.

Frozen Foods being handled by John Sutcliffe Consolidated Stevedores on the East Side Royal Dock 1961. (ABP)

CHAPTER TEN

The Company's Vessels

John Sutcliffe's intervention in 1865 assisted in creating an opportunity for the Directors of the MS&L to reconsider the direction of the Company's future operations. The report he prepared reminded the Directors that John Lumsden of Hull and his consortium were not perhaps as honourable as they appeared. He illustrated this by questioning their integrity, and highlighting the fact that their interest in undertaking the service of Anglo-French had only been revealed when the Railway Company had received Parliamentary Approval to develop its own fleet. He also analysed the possible consequences that may occur should the appointment of an independent shipping line based in Hull be supported. He concluded that shippers would prefer to use Grimsby as they would arrive up to ten hours earlier than if they were to use Hull. This being the case, it could quickly create a conflict of interest and in turn aggravate the North Eastern Railway Company (NER) who used Hull as its terminal port. The MS&L may therefore suffer, as the NER was a much larger concern which had already secured a near monopoly on trade originating from Durham, Northumberland and parts of Yorkshire.

Fortunately the Directors of the MS&L listened to the arguments presented by John Sucliffe and decided to operate their own fleet of steamships. By taking this course of action they were seen to be implementing their Parliamentary Approval as detailed in the Manchester, Sheffield & Lincolnshire (Steamboat) Act of 1864. This permitted the Company to build, buy or hire, maintain and work vessels to run from the Town or Port of Great Grimsby to Rotterdam, Antwerp, Hamburg and other Continental Ports. If however, the Company had accepted an agreement with the Hull shipowners it would have resulted in abandoning its Parliamentary powers. Negotiations were therefore able to commence with Anglo-French Shipping with a view to purchasing their fleet of vessels. Following the successful conclusion of discussions, the MS&L started operating a service to Hamburg in July of the following year.

The Railway Company could now offer an integrated package for customers using the Port. Goods delivered to the nearest railway

The Steamer 'Marylebone' operated by the Great Central Railway Company. (ABP)

station could be transported by rail wagon and steamer directly to the Continent. The twice-weekly service to Hamburg was able to provide a facility that could ship commodities out of the UK and into Germany with great ease. The benefits associated with this capability were soon realised, and in 1866 it was decided to introduce sailings to Rotterdam. In August of the following year, the service was extended to Antwerp.

The Company's objective to attract shippers from the Midlands and the North was being fulfilled. However, its competitors were also offering similar packages. This meant that potential customers could be confronted with the option of shipping their goods either via the Great Eastern Railway and Harwich, the Lancashire & Yorkshire Railway and Goole or the North Eastern Railway and Hull. It was therefore felt by all the operators that a level of control was required between these alternative routes. This resulted in protracted negotiations, which concluded in the formation of the Humber Agreement of 1855 and the

Hartlepool and Midland Agreements in the following year. These arrangements subsequently developed into the formation of the Humber Conference, which attempted to regulate the whole trade. Its objective was to create an administrative structure with a central "purse", thereby enabling all railway receipts to be divided in accordance with an agreed formula. This prevented the shipping lines creating a price war and therefore each had to secure trade by promoting its own efficiency and service.

The MS&L adopted the same policy and embarked on a campaign to publicise the benefits of the line and the facilities it could offer. This must have had the desired effect over a period of time, as it resulted in an increase in traffic. In order to satisfy this rise in demand it was eventually decided to expand its service to Hamburg and on 1December 1885 sailings were doubled to four per week. This, however, still proved insufficient and by 1 July 1891 a daily service was provided. In the meantime, the

The promenade deck on board the S.S. 'Marylebone' (ABP)

The dining saloon on board the S.S. 'Marylebone'.

MS&L Railway (Steamboats) Act of 1889 had been passed. This allowed the Railway Company to extend its operations and sail its vessels from Grimsby to Ghent, Amsterdam, Bremerhaven and to certain ports in Norway, Sweden, Denmark together with the Baltic. This was a significant period in the Company's development as it was using its fleet of 15 steamers, in conjunction with its railway and port infrastructure, to increase trade. By September 1906, the sailings between Grimsby and Rotterdam had risen from two to three per week and in the following year two new ships, the 'Marylebone' and 'Immingham' were brought into service. Incidentally, two of their predecessors, the P.S. 'Stockport' and the P.S. 'Sheffield', were blockade runners in the American Civil War prior to being purchased by the Great Central Railway.

A two-berth cabin on board the S.S. 'Marylebone' (ABP)

By 1914 the Company's fleet comprised of the following vessels:-

S.S. *'City of Bradford'* S.S. *'Accrington'*
S.S. *'Dewsbury'* S.S. *'City of Leeds'*
S.S. *'Immingham'* S.S. *'Wrexham'*
S.S. *'Lutterworth'* S.S. *'Stockport'*
S.S. *'Lincoln'* S.S. *'Nottingham'*
S.S. *'Leicester'* S.S. *'Bury'*
S.S. *'Marylebone'* S.S. *'Staveley'*
S.S. *'Chesterfield'*

When the First World War was declared in 1914, the Government requisitioned a number of the fleet, which had a detrimental effect on the Company's operations. Three further vessels were despatched, on loan, to the Great Eastern Company in order to continue its service of providing food to the Netherlands.

As a result of supporting the war effort, the GCR lost the following vessels:-

12 June 1915   S.S. 'Immingham'
Sunk in collision off Lemnos.
12 Feb 1916   S.S. 'Leicester'
Mined in English Channel.
18 May 1916   S.S. 'Chesterfield'
Torpedoed in
Mediterranean.
19 June 1918   S.S. 'Wrexham'
Wrecked in White Sea.

It was suggested that a more probable explanation for the loss of the 'Chesterfield' could have been associated with an internal explosion caused by a time bomb.

The administration of the Company's vessels was placed under the control of Mr. Alford Green, the Port Master. Mr. Hellyer was appointed the first Commercial Assistant to Mr. Green in 1903 and had full responsibility for passenger services to the Continent. This role had previously been undertaken by Messrs. Sutcliffe who had also acted as Agents for the vessels. No doubt as a result of his success in the post, Mr. Hellyer was appointed to Assistant Port Master at Immingham when the dock opened in 1912. He was succeeded as Commercial Assistant by Mr. J. H. Smith, who held the position until at least April 1921.

By the time the second MS&L Railway (Steamboats) Act was passed Mr. Green had been Port Master for five years. He was assisted by Mr. Copley, who had been appointed to the position of Marine Superintendent in 1865 and remained in the post until 1886 when he was succeeded by Captain Kennett-Hoare. Mr. T. M. Williams, who became Port Master in 1894, had taken on the title of Steamship Superintendent in 1888, when Captain Jewitt succeeded Captain Kennett-Hoare with the title of Ship's Husband and Principal Dock Master. This was regarded as an important post as it provided technical support to the Steamship Superintendent and Port Master.

The smoke room on board the S.S. 'Marylebone' (ABP)

CHAPTER ELEVEN

A Voyage to Freedom

The services provided by the Company's vessels were having a significant impact on the Port. Trade with the Continent was steadily increasing together with the number of passengers disembarking at Grimsby. Unfortunately the majority of those arriving at the Port were not visiting England to enjoy a holiday. Many were completing the first stage of a journey that would take them from their homes in Germany, Russia and Poland to a new life as far away as America.

They would initially travel to Riga, Libau, Hamburg and Rotterdam where they would pay to board ship and continue their journey. It was not uncommon for unscrupulous individuals to deceive the migrants into thinking that the cost of the passage was through to America rather than to England. Often with little money, they arrived in Grimsby unable to progress any further. Some decided to settle in the Town whilst others, determined to make their new homes in America, stayed until they could earn sufficient money to continue.

The attitude towards the Jews in Eastern Europe had been on a decline for some time, but under the rule of Tsar Alexander II (1855-1881) life had become increasingly difficult. Acts of persecution, violence and slaughter by bands of Cossacks became routine. Regrettably, the situation did not improve following the assassination of the Tsar. Anti-Jewish activities actually started to rise resulting in the vicious May Laws of 1882. These placed even greater restrictions upon their rights, liberties, areas of residence, together with their educational and professional opportunities.

Many realised that the only way to escape this suppression was to venture on a journey that would take them half way around the world. To travel directly from the Continent to America was often too expensive and therefore the only other route was across the North Sea, through England and over the Atlantic Ocean. The Great Central Railway Company could readily fulfil the first part of this epic voyage. Able to offer cheap package deals for as little as ten shillings (50 pence) the transmigrants could sail to ports including Grimsby, from where they could board trains bound for the West Coast. On arrival at Liverpool they could embark upon the final stage of their journey seeking passage to New York on the empty grain ships returning to America.

By 1879, Grimsby was experiencing between 200 and 500 immigrants per month passing through the Port. Many had endured

Migrants and transmigrants crossing the North Sea on board a Great Central Railway vessel bound for Grimsby. (NELC Welholme Galleries)

a depressing voyage living on the meagre diet of pickled herrings and black bread they had retained for the journey. They were generally accommodated below decks, possibly crowded together in a confined space where the risk of cholera and smallpox presented an additional hazard.

On arrival at the dockside they would, no doubt, have been confronted by the hustle and bustle of a busy port. Overwhelmed by their new surroundings they had to rely, to a large extent, on the local inhabitants to pursue their dream of reaching America. The assistance they required was not necessarily always available. The Town was extremely concerned about the potential outbreak of cholera and smallpox. The migrants were possible carriers of these diseases and, as such, posed a serious threat to Grimsby's ever increasing population. Dr Braxhall, in preparing his report to the local Health Board in 1887, stressed that, in his opinion, the

outbreak of cholera was more than a possibility. He highlighted that those individuals taken ill whilst on board ship would no doubt require medical attention upon their arrival at the Docks. In order to convey them to hospital, they would have to pass through the streets of Grimsby, therefore creating the potential of mass infection.

The Railway Company was trying to assist the transmigrants and immigrants where possible. It acknowledged that it had a responsibility for their onward journey, although in some cases, owing to illness or poverty, it could not always meet this obligation. However, it arranged to provide accommodation whilst the migrants were on the Dock Estate. The railway station, formerly used by Queen Victoria during her visit to the docks in 1854, was converted into a hostel. The main arch through which trains passed was sealed, and a large room was formed capable of providing shelter for up to 300

The former Royal Dock railway station and immigrants' home located on the West Side of the Dock. At the southern end of the building can be seen the outline of the arch through which the train carrying Queen Victoria would have passed during her visit to Grimsby in 1854. (ABP)

individuals. In addition, a number of smaller rooms were made available for second-class passengers. The facilities were not elegant and there was no separation between men and women. It was little more than a huge waiting room with pictures of ships adorning the walls, long tables at which food was served and the odd aspidistra to add that homely touch.

A warden supervised the management of the hostel. During the 1880's Isaac Freeman occupied this position. He would often try to offer support to the migrants. Accompanied by his wife, he would leave the old station building and wait on the quayside ready to meet new arrivals as they came ashore. Many were weary following their voyage and no doubt Isaac provided a source of reassurance, particularly as he had only become a naturalised British subject in 1871.

The line of families would make their way slowly into the great hall. Heavily bearded men, women carrying distressed babies in their arms and children dragging bundles wrapped in blankets, all seeking a place of refuge for the night. Sleeping arrangements were primitive with mattresses being laid on the floor and the tired groups finding rest as best they could. The following morning the transmigrants would depart their overnight accommodation and meander to the Docks Station. Here they continued their journey, first by train to Liverpool, then by ship across the Atlantic Ocean to America. Others stayed in this country settling in London, Leeds and Manchester. A small contingent did not leave Grimsby but decided to remain in the Town forming their own Jewish Community.

The Synagogue they established in Heneage Road still remains and many that made Grimsby their home went on to form reputable businesses in the Town.

The inside of the railway station on the Royal Dock purposely converted to accommodate the Jewish migrants and transmigrants arriving at the Port. (NELC Welholme Galleries)

CHAPTER TWELVE

The Arrival of the Butter Boats

Whilst the Company's Steamers helped to establish regular traffic for the Port, other operators were realising Grimsby's potential as an import/export centre. On 27 August 1889, Messrs. Thos. Wilson, Sons & Company, began a weekly service of passenger and cargo vessels to Copenhagen and Malmo. Departing Grimsby every Tuesday, they offered regular sailings to destinations not catered for by the Railway Company's fleet.

In recognising the strong trading links that existed between Grimsby and Scandinavia, the Company decided to substitute Halmstad for Copenhagen. This did not mean that Denmark had been dismissed from the future plans of the Company. On the contrary, the importance of the Kingdom had always been acknowledged. This was emphasised when, on 26 April 1892, a weekly service was inaugurated that left Grimsby every Saturday en route to the Danish capital.

Messrs Wilson & Company was to continue expanding their links with Northern Europe. In 1906 they established fortnightly sailings to Christiania and four years later they had developed a service between Grimsby and Riga in Latvia. However, they were not alone in appreciating the benefits of the Port.

On 16 June 1890, a vessel operator established an association with Grimsby that was to last over one hundred years. The United Steamship Company of Copenhagen set sail on its first voyage to Esbjerg carrying passengers and general cargo. The ship commissioned to ply this route was the S.S. 'Fanø'. Originally named the S.S. 'Strauss' and delivered to Norddeutscher Lloyd of Bremen in 1872, she was sold to the United Steamship Company on 31 May 1890 at a cost of 99,823 Danish Krones. By 10 June she had departed Copenhagen bound for Esbjerg where, three days later, she started

The S.S. 'Fanø' (DFDS)

her regular route between Denmark and Grimsby. Part of her cargo was to include imported livestock but the butter trade, for which the line became renowned, was not secured until some years later.

The demand for the service soon increased and by 20 May 1894 a second vessel, the S.S. 'Nidaros', had joined the S.S. 'Fanø' to provide twice-weekly sailings. This resulted in the Company being able to provide departures from Grimsby on Monday and Thursday with return voyages from Esbjerg on Tuesday and Friday.

In attempting to develop greater links with Scandinavia the Port tried to gain a portion of the trade that was passing through Newcastle from Norway. Unfortunately its efforts did not succeed, but this did not deter the Port Authority from trying to divert the Danish butter traffic from Newcastle to Grimsby. Whilst this was also unsuccessful, hopes remained high and in 1911 it continued to promote the geographical benefits of the Port in the anticipation of securing this trade in the future. Although it would appear the Port could offer exceptional facilities, thereby enabling the butter to be shipped through Grimsby, difficulties were being experienced in attracting sufficient freight for the return voyage to Denmark.

In view of this situation, it could be presumed that the United Steamship Company was not importing Danish butter into this country at that time. If this had been to the contrary, Grimsby with its already well-established services to/from Denmark would have been in an ideal position to handle the trade. It is known that Thomas Wilson, Sons & Company Limited was a tough competitor and it had regular routes between Newcastle and Denmark. It may have been this operator that had cornered the market for the butter trade thereby preventing Grimsby from attracting the traffic.

In November 1916, after being acquired by Ellerman, Thomas Wilson, Sons & Company Limited changed its name to Ellerman's Wilson Line Limited. The United Steamship Company, now known under its Danish name of Det Forenede Dampskibsselskab (DFDS), started to collaborate with its former competitor in respect of routes across the German Ocean (North Sea). It may have been at this time that Grimsby succeeded in gaining the reward it had been seeking for so long. The importation of Danish butter was eventually established as a regular commodity passing through the Port.

A priority berth was made available along the East Side of the Royal Dock, where the tubs of butter and sides of bacon could be handled with ease. They were placed in the adjoining transit sheds originally constructed during the building of the Dock in the 1850's. They were then transferred to rail wagons for their onward journey to any destination in the

Butter tubs stacked in the East Side sheds awaiting onward distribution. (ABP)

United Kingdom. The excellent railway infrastructure serving the Port provided an integral part of an encompassing package that could be offered for the handling of these commodities.

Whilst the facilities Grimsby had provided over the years had been adequate to meet the needs of conventional shipping, changes were taking place in the transportation of butter and bacon. In order to cater for the new requirements, DFDS entered into negotiations with the Port Authority during 1964 with a view to revolutionising the way in which their traffic was handled. The Company was considering the introduction of a freight system that would ensure the freshness of Danish produce transported on their vessels. It was prepared to invest considerable capital in acquiring new ships and purchasing 400 refrigerated containers capable of carrying bacon direct from the Danish abattoir to the British supermarket. However this required the assistance of the recently formed British Transport Docks Board (BTDB), to provide radical new facilities at Grimsby.

The existing berth was located on the East Side of the Royal Dock along a stretch of quay 360 feet (109.73 metres) in length. It was obvious from the discussions between DFDS and the Docks Board held in August 1964

that this would be insufficient to meet the needs they had in mind. It was therefore proposed that an additional 200 feet (60.96 metres) could be made available by demolishing part of the transit sheds to the south of the berth. A further 200 feet (60.96 metres) could also be created by removing the bicycle sheds and canteens to the north. Although the Danish representatives had not decided whether they were to proceed with the introduction of roll-on/roll-off vessels initial indications were suggesting that this would be the way forward.

By October DFDS had made its decision and announced that Grimsby would become the second of two principal ports along the East Coast handling the importation of Danish bacon. The Company had already ordered two purpose-built ferries the M.V. 'Somerset' and M.V. 'Stafford' at a cost of £900,000 each to replace the existing vessels, the M.V. 'Petunia' and M.V. 'Bellona'. These would sail twice weekly between Grimsby and Esbjerg carrying 2,000 tons (2,032 tonnes) of factory fresh bacon into the country loaded into specially refrigerated containers.

The decision to change the method of operation had been largely influenced by the Danish Bacon Board. It had been working with the producers to develop an alternative

The M.V. 'Petunia' berthed on the East Side, Royal Dock. (ABP)

The M.V. 'Somerset' arriving in the Royal Dock Basin on her maiden voyage. (ABP)

way of transporting the bacon which had, for almost 100 years, been wrapped in hessian - three sides to a single unit. This had for some time been considered unsatisfactory and after experimenting with various types of containerisation it was felt that the refrigerated trailer would be the best solution.

It was proposed that the service would be operational by the Autumn 1966. In order to ensure the fulfilment of this deadline, the Docks Board embarked upon a major construction scheme. The initial work involved the demolition of the old transit sheds. This was then followed by the improvement of the quays, the provision of a two-tier ramp for the loading/discharging of the vessels and the creation of an open storage area. In addition, extensive cabling was installed to the specially designed electrical plug points located within the

Invited dignitaries gathering for the official opening of the DFDS Terminal. (ABP)

Stilcon slabs are positioned over the area previously occupied by the original Graving Dock in order to create additional storage space. (ABP)

adjoining compound. These provided a constant source of power to the refrigeration units built into the containers, thereby allowing their continual operation whilst on the quayside awaiting onward distribution.

By November 1966 the final construction works were taking place prior to the commissioning of the Terminal. The placing of concrete fence posts around the perimeter and the relocating of buffer stops were just two of the minor items requiring completion. The project had taken approximately two years from start to finish and had cost £199,000. A joint inspection of the new facilities involving the Port Master, Peter Murdoch and representatives from DFDS and the Danish Bacon Board took place on 17 November. This provided an opportunity to finalise the arrangements for the opening on Wednesday 18 January.

Whilst it was the transportation of bacon that had influenced the implementation of new roll-on/roll-off facilities at the Port, it was not long before butter was also being handled in the same way. Although the conventional vessels such as the M.V. 'Petunia' may no longer have been required, it did not mean that Grimsby was to lose a commodity associated with the Port for upwards of 90 years. Quantities of bacon and butter continued to increase over the succeeding decades thereby resulting in the need to create additional open storage space. This was partly achieved by infilling the former dry dock and covering the area with pre-cast concrete slabs.

DFDS also realised that its existing fleet was unable to cater for the continual rising demand. It therefore embarked upon a programme of modernisation that would involve the introduction of larger vessels to the Port. However it was acknowledged that the width of the lock could prevent any further expansion in the future. Fortunately this did not deter the Company and the M.V. 'Dana Maxima' entered service between Esbjerg and Grimsby on 30 September 1978. She had been purpose-built to pass through Grimsby's lock and turn within the confines of the Dock. It was the first time that a vessel had been designed with the Port's limitations in mind and therefore she was constructed to the maximum size that could be handled.

Unfortunately the success of the service

The hull along the upper decks of the M.V. 'Dana Cimbria' overhangs the side of the lock. This creates additional space within the vessel, whilst allowing her to pass unheeded through the narrow entrance to the dock. (Chris Turner)

resulted in its eventual relocation away from the Port. The limitations of the Dock restricted the size of vessels that could be handled through the lock. The demand for ever-increasing capacity meant that anything greater in size than the 'Dana Maxima' or 'Dana Cimbria' could not clear the sides of the lock or turn within the confines of the Dock. On 28 May 1995 the Butter Boats departed the Port for the final time, leaving the DFDS Terminal to be redesignated as development land awaiting the arrival of a new user.

The Port Authority, Associated British Ports, had been aware of the situation for some time. The dimensions of the Dock were such that the trade could not remain at Grimsby if it was to develop in the future. The only alternative was for it to move and fortunately Grimsby's sister port, Immingham could, with various alterations, provide the facilities to cater for even larger ships.

The M.V. 'Dana Maxima' purpose-built to manoeuvre within the confines of the Dock. (Geoff Byman)

CHAPTER THIRTEEN

Back O'Doigs

The need to construct larger vessels has been driven by the constant demand to carry greater quantities of cargo. Over the centuries shipbuilders have continued to overcome physical constraints in order to fulfil the requirements of prospective merchants. The continual development of their skills and understanding has created a dramatic change in the way in which vessels have been constructed. The new approach to shipbuilding affected the whole industry particularly following the introduction of iron ships. Grimsby was included within this revolution, although its contribution may have been regarded as small.

Most people may recall J. S. Doig with its substantial shipbuilding and repair business on the West Side of the Royal Dock. Founded in 1904 by John Salmond Doig, it became a significant local employer trading for sixty years as a family owned business before becoming part of Ross Group in 1964. The Company continued until the end of the 1960's and represented an industry that had been associated with this area of the Dock Estate for 165 years.

The first ship repairing and building facilities outside the confines of the Dock were completed in 1804. They were located to the north of the original lock and built by Mr. J. Angerstein, one of the major shareholders of the Grimsby Haven Company, at a cost of ten

Here a steamer awaits a berth at one of the shipyards constructed at either side of the entrance to the Old Dock. (Cosalt)

thousand pounds. It was considered by Lord Yarborough that a single dry dock would prove insufficient to meet demand. He therefore decided to sell four acres of his own land to the Haven Company in 1807, for the purpose of constructing another dry dock and associated workshops. However, he appeared to be of the opinion that further facilities may be required, and retained the right to build his own ship repairing yard in the future should the need arise.

During the early years, shipbuilding was not a particularly influential business within the local economy. The first nine years, between 1804 and 1813, saw only twelve vessels being launched, all of which were of a relatively small tonnage. By 1826 the situation appears to have changed very little. Although there were now three main shipbuilders, Robert Bell, his partner William Grange, and William Elwood, their impact still remained insignificant. This could have been as a result of the size of the facilities available or perhaps the capacity of the vessels being constructed.

By 1842 the situation had started to improve. A former captain of one of the vessels of the Grimsby Shipping Company, Thomas Keetley, had formed a partnership with William Grange. Their work developed over the years but it was not until Robert Keetley succeeded his father that real progress in the local ship building industry was seen. It was during the late 1840's and through the 1850's that Robert's efforts came to the forefront. He became responsible for the construction of traditional vessels at a time when sailing ships were being challenged by steam and screw powered craft.

His facilities at Lock Hill became the regular construction site for a number of vessels commissioned by the Great Grimsby Deep Sea Fishing Company. This was an enterprise jointly sponsored by the two main Railway Companies serving the Town. The first screw driven vessel built at the yard was the 'George' in 1852. She was used to collect fish from smacks working out on the Dogger Bank and covey it back to Port, a system that later became known as "fleeting".

Unfortunately the vessel did not continue this practice for long, as it was involved in an ill-fated incident while returning from the fishing grounds. At approximately seven o'clock on the morning of 11th March 1853 she was steaming towards Spurn when, two miles from the coast, there was an explosion. Her crew of nine had, without warning, been reduced to seven. John Smith, the Mate, and John Soder had been killed instantly, whilst the remainder of the crew were rescued by a brig and ferried back to Port. A further life was lost four days later when James Smith died of his injuries sustained in the accident.

Robert Keetley continued building vessels into the 1860's but by 1870 the shipyard had been taken over by James Hallett. Originally from Hull, Hallett moved to Grimsby and set up business with his son who was also named James. They sited their operation around the entrance to the Old Dock and specialised mainly in the construction of wooden fishing smacks. The demand for these vessels had increased as a direct result of the continuing relocation of mariners from the South. The reputation of Grimsby as a newly established Fishing Port was attracting great interest and as more workers moved to the Town a greater number of smacks was required. Unfortunately, despite this apparent upsurge in trade, their venture did not have a prolonged life, and although they were employing a complement of fifty men and ten boys by 1881, the operation did not continue past the early 1880's.

During the same period another Hull born shipbuilder was making his mark at the Port. Located on the West Side of the Royal Dock, no doubt on land adjacent to the main approach to the Old Dock, James Hadfield became responsible for the construction of a number of fine wooden sailing ships. The most notable at the time was perhaps the three masted schooner 'Geraldine'.

Weighing 192 tons she sailed from London in December 1874 bound for the Congo River. On 29 January of the following year, whilst in pilotage waters, she ran aground approximately eleven miles from Port Elena. Unable to move, she attracted the attention of the local natives, who decided to attempt a raid on the schooner. Under the cover of darkness and during a thunderstorm they staged their attack. Surrounding the vessel in their canoes, they brandished various weapons as they embarked upon their mission to board the ship. The captain, Mr. Florry, immediately started to repel the boarders, and whilst discharging his revolver hit one of the natives, who dropped back into a canoe gravely injured. This resulted in the assault being abandoned and the natives

made a speedy retreat to the banks of the river, where they could take refuge in the adjoining jungle.

The crew, heeding the advice of the pilot that the natives would return, lowered the ship's boat and proceeded up river to Port Elena. Whilst the majority of the crew were able to make their escape, four local native cargo boys could not be located. When the mariners eventually returned to the 'Geraldine' on a small river steamer, the ship had been plundered and the body of one of the boys was discovered severely mutilated. Unfortunately the remaining boys were never found and the crew assumed that, in view of the quantity of blood covering the deck, they must have been murdered and their bodies thrown overboard. The remaining cargo was salvaged and loaded onto the small steamer whilst the schooner was abandoned and left to her own fate. The crew eventually returned to England arriving at Liverpool but many were suffering from yellow fever and at least one, John Williamson, died on the homeward voyage.

Many new berths were provided along the outfall to accommodate the work generated by the ship-building companies. (NELC Local Studies Library)

Although Hadfield's shipyard continued to operate until the late 1880's it was perhaps the business of Thomas Charlton that brought about the greatest change to shipbuilding in Grimsby. Born in Northumberland in 1827 he served his apprenticeship with G. & B. Stephenson of Newcastle before moving to Elswick Engineering Company and becoming involved with Sir William Armstrong. Whilst employed by Sir William he visited Grimsby to assist in the installation of the hydraulic equipment at the Dock Tower. In 1862, having previously decided to permanently move to the Town, he established his own engineering and foundry business in Church Street.

By 19 October 1864 he had secured a site to the East of the entrance of the Old Dock for shipbuilding and launched his first iron ship the 'Fruiterer'. Built for Rawson and Robinson of Hull, the vessel was intended for the Continental fruit trade but by 1871 she had been renamed and was sailing between Liverpool and Balimena in Ireland.

Charlton continued constructing a number of iron-hulled vessels in the succeeding years, one of which was commissioned by the Manchester Sheffield and Lincolnshire Railway Company. The 'Magna Charta II' was the first paddle steamer to be built in the Port and was designed to operate on the crossing from New Holland to Hull. It remained in service on this route until 1899 but by the First World War it had been withdrawn and was restricted to carrying cattle and fish traffic across the Estuary.

It was essential that the creek serving the shipyards remained free of silt at all times. In order to achieve this, a type of barge known as a scourer and nicknamed 'The Devil' was floated out at low tide towards the Humber. Propelled by the water leaving the sluice of the old lock it would travel with its paddles extended and sweep the mud from the sides of the outfall into the estuary. When it reached the West Pier at the Royal Dock Basin it was retrieved using a kedge anchor. This would involve a group of men placing the anchor into a boat and rowing up stream. They would then drop the anchor and the four individuals on the scourer would haul the barge with its paddles retracted towards the anchor. This process would be repeated until the scourer reached the old lock. (ABP)

The business continued to flourish and by the turn of the Century it had become a limited company. In 1903, following the death of Thomas, his sons, John and Thomas, took charge of the firm but by 1913 the nature of the business had changed. Decisions had been made to focus operations on ship repairing rather than shipbuilding thereby resulting in the sale of its machine shop together with the fitting shop in Church Street. The Company continued to occupy its site on the Royal Dock for a further twenty years finally ceasing business around 1934.

The Lock Hill area of the Docks appeared to be an ideal centre to locate a shipyard. The slipways could be positioned just outside the Dock from where vessels could be launched directly into the same deep water channel that presently flows from the former lock pit to the Humber. However, this did not mean that all shipbuilding was confined to the land adjacent to the Old Dock entrance. Two entrepreneurs had been operating, for some time, within the enclosed Dock, but their access to the river was more restricted than for those who had chosen Lock Hill as their base.

The end of the 19th Century and beginning of the 20th Century saw a number of new shipbuilders establishing themselves on the Dock Estate. These included the Great Grimsby Co-operative Box & Fish Carrying Company in June 1897; Schofield, Hagerup & Doughty by the end of the same year; and Charlton & Doughty in 1907. However, perhaps the company that became the most memorable of them all was that of J. S. Doig. Originally occupying a site near the dry docks at the end of Humber Bank South, it was later to relocate, expand its operation and include shipbuilding within its portfolio of activities.

A native of Dundee, John Salmond Doig, moved to Grimsby in 1899 to take up the position as foreman boilerman for the Great Grimsby Coal Salt & Tanning Company. He had previously been employed as foreman on the construction of the Forth Bridge centre pier and later as an Assistant Manager of a shipyard at Middlesbrough. He had also worked on the Thames and Humber, mainly in Hull, before settling in Grimsby.

His expertise as a shipbuilder appears to have originated from his involvement in the shipyard he founded in Montrose. No doubt he was able to use the knowledge and skills gained from this venture to establish his first business in Grimsby, which he formed in 1904. Located towards the North end of Humber Bank South, his Company was mainly involved in the repairing of vessels and provided employment for between 20 and 30 workers. By 1910 he had acquired the assets of Charlton & Doughty after their business ceased trading. This new site, adjacent to the entrance of the Old Dock, created the opportunity for Doig to set up the Strathtay Ironworks. He now had the foundation upon which he could build a self-contained shipyard in an area of the Dock Estate that had direct access to open water. Although he now had the facilities to develop his interest in shipbuilding, he concentrated his activities on the repair of small drifters and similar vessels for at least the first four years of operation.

The First World War brought additional business to the yard. It was designated as a controlled establishment, thereby allowing Naval work to be undertaken. During the succeeding years in excess of 2000 major repair contracts were carried out, including the conversion of trawlers for deployment as anti-submarine patrol craft. As the work increased the workforce also started to rise and within the war years approximately 300 were employed.

Unfortunately, work after the war started to decline. Although the business had been involved in the re-conversion of Naval vessels for civilian use, by the mid 1920's it was facing a fight for survival. The deepening economic depression meant that the Company had to seek alternative work unassociated with shipbuilding or repairing. This was achieved by tendering for projects that required steel fabrication within their construction. The Mersey Tunnel and the London Underground were two such schemes that Doig's were successful in securing.

The Company continued, where possible, to maintain its core business of shipbuilding and repairing. By 1938 it managed to acquire the lease of Charlton's yard. This property offered the potential for Doigs to handle larger ships up to 360 feet (109.73 metres) in length, on a slipway that extended into the adjoining outfall. In addition two new berths were constructed for the building of vessels, which required substantial piling work.

These new facilities must have assisted the Company, as it was able to secure a steady flow of work during the Second World War. Although John Salmond Doig died on 12 January 1940, his efforts had created a firm foundation upon which his son John Alexander Doig could build. The Company continued to prosper and during the war years it completed work on eleven wooden hulled minesweepers, 139 feet (42.37 metres) in length, six Fairmile 'B' class launches, two landing craft, four boom defence vessels and sixteen motor fishing vessels. There was also other work undertaken, including substantial refits of forty-eight Naval vessels, mainly destroyers, corvettes and sloops, together with the maintenance of coasters and minesweepers.

A Naval patrol vessel undergoing repairs in the Dry Dock at Doigs Shipyard. (Steve Pulfrey)

After the war the Company carried out conversion work on various vessels, one of the most notable being the M.S. 'Empire Sloane'. She was operated by the London Missionary Society, who required her to be brought up-to-date for missionary work in the Pacific. The yard also retained its connections with the Admiralty, who in 1951 awarded Doigs a contract to build eleven new type coastal minesweepers at a cost in the region of £3 million. The duration of the contract extended over a period of approximately six years and supported a workforce of around 250 employees.

The 'Bildesteon' was the first of the minesweepers to be launched. She was completed on 28 April 1953 and was followed in the succeeding years by the 'Edderton', 'Chrichton', 'Gavinton', 'Glasserton', 'Sullington', 'Swanston', 'Tarlton', 'Wennington', 'Belton' and 'Fiskerton'.

During the mid 1950's the Company accepted its first order to construct civilian vessels since the end of the war. The fishing vessels 'Well Bank' and 'East Bank' were to start a new chapter in the Company's development. The yard soon received orders for larger trawlers from operators including the Colne Fishing Company of Lowestoft, Lindsey Steam Fishing Company of Grimsby, Storgram Trawlers of Milford Haven and Alfred Bannister Trawlers Limited of Grimsby.

Despite the apparent buoyancy in the Company's workload the Chairman, Mr. Alex Doig, was not so confident in the yard's future. Commenting upon the receipt of an order for six Naval supply tenders in February 1963, he indicated that the yard was experiencing difficulty attracting commercial work. By July of the same year the Board of Directors recommended to the shareholders that they accept an offer made by Ross Group. This was subsequently ratified and in January 1964 J. S. Doig Limited ceased being a family owned concern.

The business continued to operate for some time attracting various orders but the

J.S. Doig Limited carried out substantial work for the Port's fishing fleet. The photograph shows the 'Ross Fame' on the Company's slipway undergoing refurbishment work. (Steve Pulfrey)

British shipbuilding industry in general was experiencing a steady decline. Increased foreign competition, combined with the forced exclusion of the British fishing fleet from Icelandic waters, eventually ended shipbuilding at the Lock Hill outfall. In January 1969 Ross Group sold its other shipyard, Cochrane & Sons of Selby to Drypool Engineering & Dry Dock Company Limited. During the same year the facilities at Doigs were allowed to run down and a piece of history spanning 165 years finally came to an end.

Many of the buildings remained standing into the 1970's. The canteen, together with the large engineering workshop complete with its overhead gantry crane, were finally cleared in the late 1970's or early 1980's. The office building was not demolished until the 1990's and accommodated such businesses as Hull Gate Shipping Company, Community Rural Aid (CRA) and Dyson Engineering. Tyup Shipping occupied the small office to the South of the main building. The gentleman who operated the Company was Mr. Hagerup who possibly was a descendant of Scholfield, Hagerup & Doughty, previous shipbuilding occupants of the site

Taken from the Dock Offices in the early 1970's, the former buildings of Doig's Shipyard can be seen in the background before the site was eventually cleared. (ABP)

CHAPTER FOURTEEN

The War Years

J. S. Doig Limited made significant contributions towards the protection of the Kingdom during both World Wars. Whilst it was constructing Naval vessels to guard our shores, the Port of Grimsby had been preparing to play its part in the conflicts. During July 1913 the Royal Dock Basin had been involved in Naval manoeuvres on the Humber. The "Red" forces commanded by Vice Admiral Sir John Jellicoe were attacking the "Blue" forces under the direction of Admiral Sir George Callaghan. Destroyers, cruisers and submarines supported each group, but the "Red" force also contained three battalions of infantry in addition to one thousand Royal Marines. It is therefore not surprising that Grimsby was "captured" by the invading force.

These exercises not only provided valuable experience in acting out various military strategies but also for demonstrating the ways in which the Port would have to respond in the event of an invasion. Although the threat of attack existed during the First World War it was not as great as that experienced some twenty years later.

Grimsby was not unaccustomed to entertaining Naval visits. The Port had, since at least 1908, been a base for British submarines. Its favourable geographical location in relation to the North Sea together with the availability of ample berthing space in Alexandra Dock made it ideal for the purpose. However, perhaps the most important involvement of the Port in assisting Naval activities remained one of the best-kept secrets.

Situated on the West Pier of the Royal Dock Basin a group of insignificant buildings

One of the many submarines that visited the Port rounds the Coaling Jetty heading for Alexandra Dock. (NELC Welholme Galleries)

The Radio Station located on the West Pier that was operated by the Admiralty during the First World War.
(David Hopcroft)

was helping to influence the outcome of the war. Accommodated in three disused passenger railway carriages, placed end to end, the Admiralty could monitor and communicate with vessels in the Humber District. The radio station was equipped with a Naval 2 kilowatt spark transmitter through which a communiqué was issued in 1919 for the British fleet to cease hostilities. In 1920 its operation was transferred to the Post Office together with the stations at Wick and Portpatrick. Although it remained in existence for some years after the transfer it was eventually replaced by a new "Humber" Radio Station with up-to-date equipment located at Trusthorpe to the South of Mablethorpe.

The development of warfare had advanced significantly during the inter-war period. The London & North Eastern Railway, together with the Government, were however aware that the impending conflict with Germany would require a totally different tactical approach in comparison to the First World War. A greater emphasis would no doubt be placed on the use of air power and with this in mind they had, for some time, been implementing various methods of defence. Air Raid Precaution (ARP) schemes had already been introduced in June 1937 and wardens were based in the cellars of the Dock Offices. This provided excellent accommodation in the event of an attack as the solid brick walls and concrete floors were approximately 14 inches (35.56 centimetres) thick. In addition, the temporary measures for the protection of staff, structures and plant, mainly by the use of sandbagging, were carried out during the crisis of September 1938. These schemes were then revised in 1939 in order to comply with Civil Defence Act authorised in August of the same year.

In August 1936 the Grimsby & Immingham Port Emergency Committee was formed under the Chairmanship of the Port Master. This body was granted extensive powers as it included individuals representing Coastal Shipping and Short Sea Shipping Control; Home Trade and Overseas Trade; Customs; Naval and Military Authorities; US Army Authorities; the National Dock Labour Corporation; road transport; oil and traders of the Port. Under the authority of the Minister of War Transport and the Control of Traffic at Ports Order, 1939, it was assigned full powers to regulate the loading and discharging of shipping at Grimsby & Immingham. It also ensured that the transit sheds, warehouses and quays were cleared as soon as possible thereby increasing the turnaround of vessels.

The Committee was fully aware of the potential vulnerability of the Port and by 1940 schemes were in place for the immobilisation of the lock gates, bridges, cranes and dredging craft. In the event of the Docks being seized by the enemy, selected individuals had been instructed to remove or destroy essential machinery parts together with any plans that may reveal information relating to main services on the Estate. The Admiralty, as a precautionary measure, had located explosives under the jetties at the entrance to the Dock. Demolition charges had also been placed at the lock gates, but these were subsequently removed when the Railway Company provided concrete blocks to obstruct the operation of the gates. In addition, special ships were held ready to move into the locks for sinking should the Port be seen to be in danger of capture.

The Port was seen as a substantial military target and therefore necessary steps had to be taken in order to maintain its security. By November 1939, the whole of the Dock Estate had been classified as a 'Protected Place' as detailed in the Defence Regulations of the same year. A greater number of police were drafted into the Port area and a permit system was introduced to regulate casual visitors. Gun positions were selected and work started on the construction of concrete bases for the anti-aircraft defences. The Admiralty also moved a number of its Naval guns onto site in order to increase the resistance against the enemy.

The Port became a strategic base for the armed services. The Royal Air Force established a depot for ship barrage balloons close to the entrance to the Fish Docks and the Navy formed a Kite Balloon Section. During 1940 one of the New Holland to Hull paddle steamers was requisitioned and based in Grimsby in order to be used as a Royal Navy balloon tender.

The regulations implemented by the Government not only catered for the protection of the Port but also the workers employed on the Dock Estate. The construction of air raid shelters commenced in August 1939 and were substantially completed during the early part of the following year. They were mainly built above ground with brick walls and a concrete roof. Each shelter had the ability to accommodate up to fifty persons. A number still remain, one of the most prominent being that to the West of the Dock Offices adjacent to the electrical substation.

Despite the continued threat of attack the Port was able to work throughout 24 hours where necessary. In order for this to be achieved approved lighting had to be provided at all berths. This needed to be sufficient to meet the requirements of both the cranes and the ships. The reduced level of illumination, however, often caused problems and at times it was impossible to distinguish between the edge of the quay and the adjoining water area. To minimise accidents the Port Authority painted all quay edges with a black and white chequered line and other obstacles including bollards were painted white. Although these precautions were undertaken it did not prevent 112 individuals falling into the Dock, of which 29 drowned

Enemy action was directly responsible for the death of three Port Authority employees whilst carrying out their duties and a further nine were reported injured. By June 1944 workers had encountered over 700 air raid warnings at level 'Red' and the Port had

sustained substantial damage. The greatest devastation appears to have occurred on the Fish Docks in 1943. On 14 June the whole superstructure of the timber fish markets, from Henderson Jetty to the Swing Bridge across the cutting between No. 1 & 2 Fish Docks, was completely destroyed by fire. During the following month the South Market at No. 2 Fish Dock experienced extensive damage to the roof and glazing.

Although the Commercial Dock did not appear to have suffered to the same extent, certain areas of the Estate were affected. Rail tracks towards the West Marsh were hit on 23 February 1941, together with a 40 foot (12.19 metres) section of the 7 foot (2.13 metres) diameter Pyewipe Sewer. This eventually

GB 6, BB 14, Nr. 7: Fischereihafen von Grimsby.
Auf der rechten Bildseite unterteiltes Hafenbecken mit Fischdocks und Trockendocks für Fischdampfer und Küstenfahrzeuge. Im linken Hafenrand Fischhallen mit 31 000 qm nutzbarer Bodenfläche. Im Vordergrund rechts Hafenbahnhof mit Gleisführungen zu den einzelnen Hafenbecken.

An aerial view of the Royal and Fish Docks taken by the German Luftwaffe before the Second World War. (Grimsby Evening Telegraph)

collapsed and resulted in the flooding of parts of Cromwell Road. It was the main outfall serving the western side of the Town and as a result of its destruction sewerage could not be discharged into the River. Four days later Alexandra Dock took a direct hit destroying areas of permanent way, thereby causing disruption to rail traffic using the Port.

Repairs to damaged structures were undertaken when possible, but as far as the reconstruction of the Fish Markets was concerned, this had to be left until after the war. The same philosophy was adopted in respect of No. 8 bonded warehouse which was also destroyed in the same attack.

Trade passing through the Port was drastically reduced during the war years. In 1938 total traffic, excluding coal and fish, had reached 481,166 tons (488,865 tonnes) but by 1940 this had decreased to 104,740 tons (106,416 tonnes). The River Humber was frequently subjected to mining activity by enemy aircraft during 1940 and 1941. This necessitated the closure of the Port on a number of occasions thereby resulting in the downturn in traffic. Certain goods, mainly those of a flammable nature, were difficult to handle, as they could not be stored on the Dock Estate. All timber, for example, was dispersed to inland destinations in order to reduce the risk of fire at the Port.

It was also a period of change for the employment of labour. A large percentage of the male workforce had joined the armed services, leaving a void in the working population. The Port Master's Department experienced a decrease in staff of 154 men and 7 women, whilst the Chief Engineer and the Docks Machinery Engineer's Departments lost a further 142 individuals. Women quickly started to take over the roles previously occupied by the men. They became shunters, motor drivers, signalwomen, platelayers and tradesmen's labourers, as well as clerical staff.

A flotilla of craft carrying troops, crosses the Royal Dock Basin, during Naval manoevres in July 1913. (NELC Local Studies Library)

At the same time there was a change taking place in the way in which dock workers were employed. In the past, Port Transport Workers had been engaged on a casual basis. However, as a result of the implementation of the Essential Work (Dock Labour) Order on 30 March 1942 they were placed under the control of the National Dock Labour Corporation Limited. This organisation was responsible for the allocation of labour to the various employers on the days they were required for work. No man could be employed loading/discharging a vessel unless he was registered under the scheme. These individuals later became known as Registered Dock Workers or 'Dockers' for short. The National Dock Labour Corporation Limited eventually became the National Dock Labour Board and remained in existence until it was disbanded by the Conservative Government, under the leadership of Margaret Thatcher.

The effects of decasualisation of labour, initially introduced to assist the war effort, had a lasting impact on all the ports. The Essential Work Order gave the Port Transport Worker a guaranteed weekly wage. Each man was placed into one of three groups, A, B or C, according to his physical capabilities. Category A men were guaranteed payment for eleven half shifts, whilst category B were entitled to nine and category C six. These entitlements were available provided they reported for duty. The individuals did not have to be engaged in any work in order to receive the guaranteed payment. This practice remained in place until the National Dock Labour Scheme was abolished in 1989.

The war formed a sense of solidarity amongst employees. They were working together to ensure that the country could continue to operate under the difficult situation it had to endure. This unified approach was evident on the Dock Estate and in recognition of the contribution made in maintaining the Port's operational capabilities awards were bestowed on the following individuals:-

Port Master's Department
C. H. Wilkinson
Driver Loco Dept., Grimsby
Awarded MBE for services in connection with salvage of vessels.

R. Price
Transport Worker, Grimsby
Awarded BEM for services in connection with bomb reconnaissance

F. Marshall
Transport Worker, Grimsby
Awarded BEM for outstanding leadership in ship working.

W. Moore
Transport Worker, Grimsby
Awarded BEM for outstanding leadership in ship working.

Chief Engineer for Docks.
A. L. Jackson
Draughtsman, Grimsby
Awarded BEM in recognition of services as Bomb Reconnaissance Officer.

Docks Machinery Engineer.
J. Great
Engineman, Slipways Grimsby
Awarded BEM for services in connection with salvage of vessels.

J. T. W. Last
Lamp Attendant, Grimsby
(assigned to RAF) Mentioned in Despatches

The Railway Company's staff were not the only individuals to be honoured as a result of their efforts during the war. Grimsby had been the largest minesweeping base in the country, and had seen 39 of its vessels sunk by enemy action in the Humber and its approaches. Manned by the Royal Naval Patrol Service (RNPS), the fleet was a combination of purpose-built minesweepers and converted trawlers that had been commandeered by the Admiralty. During the years of conflict they tried to ensure that the convoys of merchant ships received a safe passage through waters mined by the Germans. The work was extremely demanding and on one occasion, whilst hastily manoeuvring two of the craft side by side within the confines of the small lock, they became wedged and had to be forced apart. However, despite this unfortunate incident the endeavours of the minesweeper squadron were highly commendable and in recognition

of their achievements a commemorative plaque was located on the West Side of the Dock Tower.

In recent years the RNPS Veterans, under the Chairmanship of Tom Walkley, approached the Port Authority with regard to the possibility of erecting a more prominent memorial. Associated British Ports seriously considered the request and identified a site to the west of the lock. In August 2001 the Port Director, Dennis Dunn, unveiled a grey granite tablet at a special ceremony, thereby providing a new record of remembrance to mark the work of the Squadron. The following year a further honour was bestowed on the local men and women who served in the Patrol Service, when they received the Freedom of the Borough of Great Grimsby.

The unveiling ceremony attended by, from left, Pauline Dunn, Tom Walkley and Dennis Dunn. (Tom Walkley)

CHAPTER FIFTEEN

Post War Changes

The majority of the work undertaken after the war was restricted to rectifying the damage that had resulted from six years of conflict. The main infrastructure at Grimsby had fortunately remained intact and the Docks could continue to operate with minimal additional capital investment.

The Port appeared to change very little during the immediate post-war years. It remained under the control of the London & North Eastern Railway Company (LNER) and was administered from the Dock Offices, located adjacent to Cleethorpe Road. The Government, however, was in the process of making sweeping changes that would affect many of the country's principal industries.

As a result of the Transport Act 1947 the railway ports were nationalised and Grimsby, together with Immingham, Hull and Goole, was placed under the jurisdiction of the British Transport Commission (BTC). The four main dock systems on the Estuary were consolidated into the Humber Ports group and placed under the control of the Chief Docks Manager, Hull. He was responsible, in turn, to the Docks & Inland Waterways Executive, a division of the BTC.

The new structure within the ports did not necessarily have any detrimental effect upon the operation of Grimsby's Commercial Docks. The Port Master now reported to the Chief Docks Manager rather than directly to Liverpool Street, as had previously been the case under the LNER. However he continued to retain his direct responsibility for the overall control of the Port. This included the re-establishment of trade, which had been severely disrupted during the war years.

The volume of traffic passing over the quays did not really recover until the early 1950's. Some commodities including those handled by DFDS were still below pre-war levels in 1955. It was fortunate that a few local industries were experiencing an upturn in business. Peter Dixon & Son Limited, for example, was importing 130,000 tons (132,080 tonnes) of Woodpulp per annum

Wood pulp bound for Peter Dixon & Son Ltd. being discharged to rail transport on the West Side, Royal Dock. (ABP)

from Finland and Norway for use in its paper making process in Grimsby and Oughtibridge near Sheffield. Sawn timber and pitwood were also experiencing an increase with approximately 80,000 tons being handled during the mid 1950's.

Whilst imports were only rising steadily certain outward traffics were achieving more rapid growth. Over one and a quarter million tons of coal had been shipped through the Port between 1953 and 1954 which represented the best figures since 1931. A large proportion of this trade was for coastwise destinations including power stations operated by the Central Electricity Authority. Exports of coal fluctuated considerably in response to changes in production levels and internal consumption. Fortunately the volume shipped for export was only seen to be a small proportion of the total handled by the two main coal hoists in the Royal Dock. In addition, iron and steel,

together with machinery, were also proving to be valuable export commodities for the Port.

As trade started to increase the Port Authority embarked upon a programme of redevelopment. One of the first schemes to be progressed was the reconstruction of the West Pier of the Royal Dock Basin. Originally built in 1851, it was extensively restructured in 1896 and further strengthened in 1933. However, by the end of 1951 the condition of the timberwork had deteriorated to such an extent that major refurbishment was required. Before the project could be finalised the Pier was subjected to severe damage during the great storm of 31 January 1953 and the 1,100 feet (335.24 metres) structure was breached in two places. In order to rectify the destruction that had occurred it was decided to progress with the total replacement of the existing structure. The work involved the removal of the remaining sections of the

Two vessels load simultaneously on either side of the Coaling Jetty during the 1960's. (NELC Local Studies Library)

A panoramic view of the Coaling Jetty showing the covered conveyor system together with the numerous sidings that ran along the back of the quays on the West Side of the Royal Dock. circa 1950's. (NELC Local Studies Library)

Pier, the demolition of the adjoining timber quay and the provision of new facilities for the berthing of paddle steamers. The new jetty was then constructed by locating a reinforced concrete walkway on piled bents 12 feet 6 inches (3.81 metres) apart over a total length of approximately 1,100 feet (335.28 metres). The first section that lay alongside the old outfall channel measured 450 feet (137.16 metres), with the remaining part running at an angle out into the River towards the North Sea. The work was eventually completed in June 1960 at a cost of £206,000.

Clearing a spillage of coal in 1954. (Grimsby Evening Telegraph)

Passengers wait to board the P.S. 'Wingfield Castle' before departing on one of her Summer trips from the Royal Dock Basin to Spurn. The Dock Master's house, located to the west of the large lock at the Royal Dock, can be seen to the left of the photograph. (NELC Local Studies Library)

By 1963 the operation of the Port had been placed under the control of the British Transport Docks Board (BTDB). This was a nationalised body created as a result of the dissolution of the BTC. Unlike its predecessor it was only responsible for the ports within its jurisdiction, the railways and the inland waterways having been separated into their own independent organisations.

It was following the formation of the BTDB that a greater emphasis started to be placed on the future development of Grimsby's Commercial Docks. Whilst the work on the West Pier was necessitated as a result of the combined effects of age, marine borers and the stress of weather, the modernisation and re-cranage of the West Side of the Royal Dock evolved from the need to update existing facilities. The project, which cost £401,000 to accomplish, was divided into two parts with the civil engineering work commencing first. This catered for the provision of flush concrete quay surfaces adjacent to the berths, improvements to the layout of rail tracks, upgrading of road access and modernisation of the transit sheds. As the structural work was completed arrangements were then made to install three new dual seven-and-a-half/three ton cranes and eight separate three ton cranes. The whole scheme was finished by March 1967, some five months later than expected.

The general attitude to renew the infrastructure provided created the opportunity to attract additional trade through the Port as a result of the facilities it could now offer. Unfortunately this approach did not target any specific traffic and could have been seen, at the time, as a costly exercise to encourage any cargoes that may have been available. However, this is not to say that the capital investment incurred was not required. The Port was in need of radical improvement but in the mid 1960's the Port

Master, Mr. Peter Murdoch and his staff adopted an alternative approach in the way trade could be secured. It was realised that if the Port Authority was able to provide purpose-built facilities to meet the needs of a user or potential user, it may be possible to enter an arrangement whereby the client would trade with the Port for a agreed period of time. This would create stability for the client and guaranteed income for the Port.

One of the first Companies to benefit from this approach was DFDS, who in 1966 moved their operations to a newly constructed roll-on/roll-off terminal on the East Side, Royal Dock. Following a continued increase in traffic the facilities were expanded, the capital

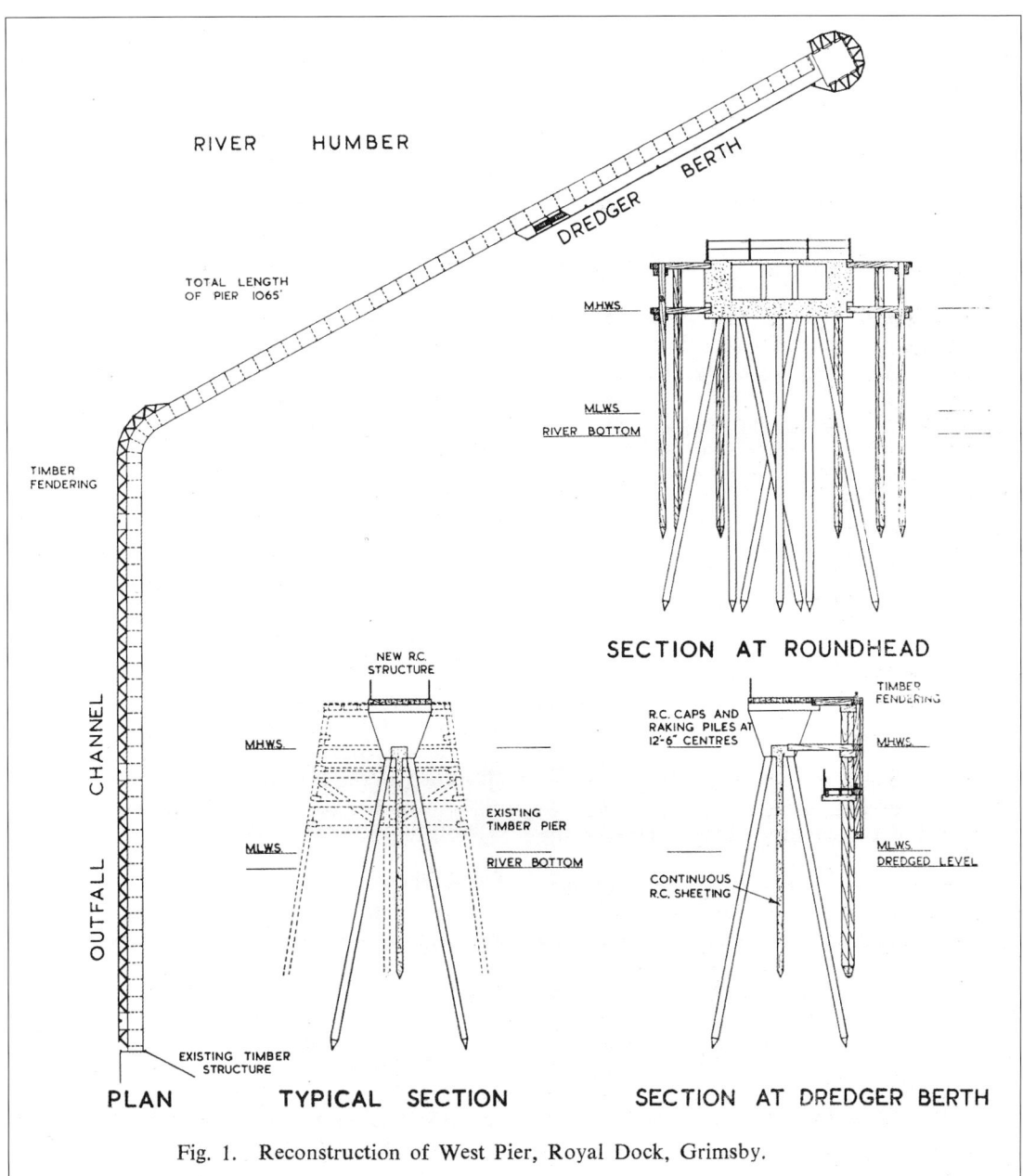

Fig. 1. Reconstruction of West Pier, Royal Dock, Grimsby.

Engineer's plans showing the reconstruction of the West Pier in 1960. (ABP)

expenditure again being financed by the BTDB. This philosophy was developed further and as a result the Port continued to experience a resurgence in trade.

In addition to creating accommodation for regular shipping lines, the Port Authority was asked, towards the end of the 1960's, to assist in providing a suitable berth for a much smaller vessel. A group of Humberside businessmen had decided to launch a hovercraft service that would link Grimsby, Immingham and Hull. They formed a Company, Humber Hoverferry Limited, and announced on 13 April 1968 that a new vessel had been ordered at a cost of £70,000. It would provide a regular service between Grimsby and Hull operating six trips a day in each direction, with a journey time of approximately twenty-five minutes. The hovercraft was designed to carry thirty-six passengers with a single fare in the region of ten shillings (50 pence). Following a period of trials together with special promotional

excursions to the Spurn Anchorage it commenced operation from the Queen's Steps at the Royal Dock Basin on 17 February 1969. The 'Mercury' left her moorings at 8.40am bound on her inaugural flight for Victoria Pier, Hull. The following month the 'Minerva' joined the service thereby substantially increasing the number of crossings that could be provided. The combined schedule was initially well supported, but unfortunately this was not to last. A series of incidents followed that started to raise questions regarding the reliability of the service. A trawl net caught around the starboard propeller of the 'Mercury' which resulted in the loss of a number of crossings. The 'Minerva' then struck the Royal Dock Basin on 10 October, almost sinking after she had been badly holed. A few days later the manufacturers, Hovermarine, went into liquidation and the timetable had to be suspended after 21 October 1969, never to be resumed.

The renewal of the quay surface and improvements to the transit sheds, West Side, Royal Dock. (ABP)

CHAPTER SIXTEEN

A Gift from Norway

It is fortunate that the Port Authority's efforts to accommodate customers' needs have not always ended in failure. Towards the end of the 1970's one of Grimsby's regular shipping lines was entering a period of change. Nordenfjeldske Dampskibsselskabs (NFDS) had formed a partnership with the Bergen Line (BDS) to establish a roll-on/roll-off service into Grimsby thereby expanding the volume of traffic it was carrying on its conventional vessels. In fulfilling this objective, representatives from the Company approached the BTDB with a view to seeking support for the project. Following intense negotiations a scheme was agreed whereby the Company's operations would relocate to new purpose-built facilities within the Royal Dock.

The outcome of the discussions proved to be in the interests of both parties. NFDS started trading with the Port in 1948 and the inability of the BTDB to assist the Company

Grimsby's annual Christmas tree arrives from Norway on 13 December 1967 aboard the M.V. 'Torfinn Jarl'. For the first time it was to be transported into Town by lorry rather than by a horse-drawn cart. The 33ft tree, which was erected at the River Head, was a present from two Norwegian Companies, the NFDS shipping line of Trondheim and a paper manufacturer at Ranheim. The Mayor of Grimsby, Ald. A. H. Chatteris receives the gift on behalf of the Town accompanied by, from left to right: Mr. A. F. Watson, The Deputy Town Clerk; I. Danielsen, the ship's Captain and Mr. R. Turrell, a representative of the ship's agents, Ed. Bannister Ltd. (Grimsby Evening Telegraph)

in supporting its proposals could have resulted in the traffic moving away from Grimsby. This, in turn, would have de-stabilised the recognised schedules NFDS had created over the years between Norway and England, thereby possibly resulting in a decline in business.

Its links with the Port had originally been established on the back of Grimsby's renowned reputation for the handling of fish. The Norwegians, wishing to export their fresh and chilled fish, had no hesitation in allowing their valuable commodity to be despatched to such a distinguished destination. NFDS was commissioned to transport the cargo and its first vessel berthed in the Royal Dock on 19 January 1948. The M.V. 'Otter Jarl' was an American ship, built in 1929. She was consigned to Ed. Bannister & Company Limited who had been appointed agents for the line, with John Sutcliffe & Son (Grimsby) Limited acting as stevedores and cargo brokers. She was later joined by the M.V. 'Guttorm Jarl' which enabled the Company to operate a fortnightly schedule incorporating one call a week at Grimsby. The service soon became locally known as the 'Jarl Line' after the name of its vessels. The Company had

adopted a policy to honour the old provincial Earls or 'Jarls' of Norway and in doing so, the 'Sigurd Jarl', 'Sote Jarl', 'Toste Jarl', 'Frode Jarl' and 'Atle Jarl' were to become some of the regular visitors to the Port.

Although trade was initially slow to develop, 9,500 tons (9,652 tonnes) of Norwegian fish was recorded as being landed in Grimsby in 1949 via the Jarl Line. Cargoes continued to rise over subsequent years, but in general this was a one-way traffic with the vessels returning to Norway light. John Sutcliffe & Son realised that potential existed for the empty ships to be used for the transportation of exports to Norway. Further investigation revealed that through their network of branches they could attract traffic for the Jarl Service, thereby creating export trade for NFDS.

The Service steadily expanded and by the mid 1950's it was decided to replace the 'Otter Jarl' with new reefer vessels, the first of which was delivered in 1956. Six years later a further two had joined the fleet, the M.V. 'Sigurd Jarl' and the M.V. 'Sote Jarl', both of which were lengthened in 1973 in order to meet increasing demand. By 1976 the M.V. 'Atle Jarl' had been introduced into the

Cargoes being loaded onto road transport ready for onward distribution after arriving from Norway on the 'Jarl Service' operated by NFDS - Grimsby Norway Line. (ABP)

The M.V. 'Astrea' berthed at the new Nor-Cargo Terminal, East Side, Royal Dock, constructed in 1979. (ABP)

schedule and an office established in the Town under the name of Grimsby Norway Line, which was a wholly owned subsidiary of NFDS. These events came at a time when the benefits of North Sea oil was improving trade between Norway and Britain, which in turn provided the opportunity for the Company to further develop its own business.

By 2 April 1979 the Board of Directors of the BTDB had approved the capital investment required to create a new roll-on/roll-off berth for the service which was to be operated under a joint partnership between NFDS and BDS. The work involved the construction of a roll-on/roll-off ramp, the provision of an open storage area, the erection of a new transit shed and the creation of an access road to the Terminal. Tenders were invited for the contract and work commenced later that year at a cost of approximately £670,000. When the work was completed the Company, now re-named Nor-Cargo Limited,

moved across the Dock from its original No. 11 berth on the West Side to No. 6 berth on the East Side.

As a result of the new facilities the volume of trade continued to rise. Eventually the Terminal became too small to meet the extra demand and in 1994 the Port Authority embarked upon another phase of expansion. The existing transit shed was extended and a further area of open storage adjacent to the Union Dock was provided at a total cost of £475,000.

The close association that has developed between Grimsby and Norway as a result of the service provided by Nor-Cargo and its predecessors has been marked by the arrival of the Town's annual Christmas tree. A special gift from the Norwegian people, the tree has, for many years, been officially received by the Mayor of Grimsby from the captain of a Nor-Cargo or NFDS vessel.

CHAPTER SEVENTEEN

The Final Decades of the Century

Whilst NFDS and its successors were provided with the necessary support to relocate their operations in order to meet an objective, this initiative was not restricted to existing trade. During the early 1970's local management received an approach from a Company that was considering Grimsby as a potential centre for the handling of its traffic.

In order to demonstrate the willingness of the Port to consider any new trade, representatives of the BTDB met the Company concerned. After listening to the customer's proposals it was acknowledged that if the potential traffic was to pass through the Port substantial investment would be required. However, this did not deter either party and it was decided to examine the matter further.

Volkswagen (GB) Limited was seeking to establish a northern port of entry into this country for its cars and light commercial vehicles. These were to include Audi in addition to those manufactured under its own marque. At the same time the timber trade that had been synonymous with Alexandra Dock, was slowly relocating off the Dock Estate. The importers had been experiencing rising costs and, by moving their businesses away from the Port, the expense of employing registered dock workers as part of their workforce could be removed. This created large areas of vacant land adjacent to the quays ideally suited for open storage.

Local management realised that the possibility of securing Volkswagen to the Port would not be an easy task. Whilst providing a site for the storage of vehicles would not prove a problem, the ability to accommodate the vessels was a different matter. Substantial reconstruction work would be required. The

Union Dock had originally been constructed to permit sailing ships to pass from the Royal Dock into the Alexandra Dock. The new car carrying vessels had a much wider beam and therefore the width of the Cutting had to be greatly increased. In addition a purpose-built berth was required at the far end of the West Arm of Alexandra Dock in order to enable the vehicles to be driven straight off the ship and onto the quayside.

Intense negotiations between representatives of the BTDB and Volkswagen (GB) Limited were eventually concluded, and as a result, the Directors of the Board granted the necessary authority for the work to commence. By December 1973 tenders were invited for the widening of the Union Dock Cutting, the provision of a roll-on/roll-off ramp, the re-alignment of the roadway to the rear of the Cross Berth and the construction of a pump house, together with a dam, close to the junction of the South Arm and the River Freshney.

The work made steady progress and was completed in time for the first vessel, the M.V. 'Ramsgate', to berth at the new facilities in May 1975. This event was to mark an association that would continue to develop over the next twenty-five years. Trade soon started to increase and by 1979, 30,000 vehicles per annum were being imported through the Terminal, with an average of two vessels per week arriving from the German port of Emden.

The Government's decision to privatise the BTDB in 1983 created the opportunity for its successor, Associated British Ports (ABP), to invest in its facilities at Grimsby. In addition to refurbishing its existing infrastructure the Company was able to provide even greater assistance in fulfilling the requirements of its

Looking towards the East Side of the Royal Dock as work is about to commence on the widening of the Union Dock. The bridge that carried both rail and road traffic was to be removed and replaced with a floating pedestrian pontoon. (ABP)

customers. In this respect ABP had, by 1989, recognised that the single roll-on/roll-off ramp constructed 14 years earlier, was incapable of meeting anticipated demand. It was therefore agreed that two new berths should be built in the West Arm of Alexandra Dock at a cost of £1.1 million. Work commenced in 1990 and was finished within a two-year period.

The new facilities did not only benefit the vessels being used by Volkswagen (GB) Limited, but also assisted Grimsby in securing the exports of Toyota cars. Transporters leaving Burnaston near Derby could travel along motorways and dual carriageways directly from the manufacturing plant into the ten acre Terminal on Alexandra Dock. In addition, vessels arriving at the Port to discharge vehicles produced by Volkswagen

were able to return to the Continent with Toyota cars. The two Companies soon started to seek additional storage space. By 1994 a further five acres were developed by Toyota and at the same time VAG (UK) Limited decided to move its entire operation onto the Dock Estate from its previous location on the South Humberside Industrial Estate.

In order to accommodate VAG's operations, a former infill site to the north of Alexandra Dock was levelled and surfaced. This created 50 acres (20.24 hectares) of open storage capable of providing a holding area for approximately 10,000 vehicles. The project, which cost £3.55 million to complete, assisted in enhancing Grimsby's image as a significant vehicle handling centre. In the region of 50% of all Audi/Volkswagen cars registered in the UK entered the country through the new Terminal.

The South Arm of Alexandra Dock extends towards the Town centre creating a vast water area for the handling of vessels bringing timber to the Port. The area between the Dock and Alexandra Road, which can be seen heading away from the West Arm, was leased by the timber importers including the Grimsby Timber Company, Marshall, Knott & Barker, Richardson & Company (Grimsby) Limited, and Wintringham & Son Limited. In the foreground can be seen Brick Pit Sidings and to the left of the photograph the outfall that formed the original entrance to the Old Dock. (ABP)

The car traffic was not the only trade to be attracted to Alexandra Dock. Following the demise of the National Dock Labour Scheme, two local businessmen were seeking to establish a shipping firm on the Humber. They discussed their proposals with representatives of ABP who highlighted the regeneration that was taking place within Alexandra Dock. As a result of further negotiations they decided to locate their operational base in Grimsby and by May 1990 ABP had authorised the development of a new Terminal at a cost in excess of £1.7 million. The 10 acre (4.05 hectares) site on the North Side of the Dock incorporated a new 150m by 40m quay together with transit shed accommodation, the latter being funded by the Operating Company. The work was completed on schedule with the first vessel being handled at the new berth on 20 November 1990. During the following year the Operators, Freshney Cargo Services Limited (Freshney) achieved a throughput of 138,800

tonnes which has subsequently risen to over 462,000 by the end of the Century.

The increase in trade has resulted in the need for continued investment both by ABP and Freshney. New transit sheds have been erected and additional storage areas constructed to the west, north and east of the original Terminal. The Company, under the leadership of Malcolm Pattison and Michael Czartowski has formed a close association with Barrow Haven Shipping Services who, in turn, has re-introduced imported timber back into Alexandra Dock.

During the past twenty-five years Grimsby's Commercial Docks have experienced a dramatic change. A number of the old established traffics have departed but these have been replaced by new services bringing alternative trade to the Port. Amongst the new arrivals have been the British Antarctic Survey vessels. These provide support for the scientists who undertake research work in the Southern

The final sections of the Union Dock have still to be removed but the pedestrian pontoon, designed by Mr. D. Hewson, is already in place. (ABP)

The pumping station across the South Arm of Alexandra Dock under construction. (ABP)

Hemisphere. They usually leave Grimsby during the Autumn and travel to the South Pole in time to arrive for its Summer period. As Winter approaches they make their return journey, which often creates a sense of a home-coming for those families who have congregated on the quayside to welcome the 'John Biscoe', 'Bransfield', 'James Clark Ross' or 'Ernest Shackleton' back into Port.

Although these vessels have, over the years, been a regular sight in the Port they have not commanded the same visual impact as that of the car ferries. Berthed adjacent to the A180 visitors travelling along the dual carriageway have a clear view of their superstructure above the lines of cars in the adjoining compound. Their huge capacity enables each vessel to transport, on average,

700 cars in one shipment and with at least one arriving each day substantial storage space is required. The present combined area occupied by Toyota and the Volkswagen Group is in the region of 125 acres (50.59 hectares) and with approximately 200 vehicles per acre, it is possible, at full capacity, to store 26,000 vehicles on the site.

Whilst Grimsby's ability to attract the car trade may have been heralded as a success story for the Town, it would be unwise to allow past achievements to overshadow the work required to ensure that the Commercial Docks continue to develop in the future. It is with this in mind that the Port Authority has endeavoured to provide up-to-date facilities for those wishing to establish trading links with the Port. This has often involved

The M.V. 'Ramsgate', the first vessel to discharge Volkswagen vehicles at Alexandra Dock, enters the newly widened Union Dock Cutting. (ABP)

Fig 82. Looking from the western end of the West Arm, Alexandra Dock towards the Freshney Terminal. (Geoff Byman)

implementing changes that have not always been favourably accepted. However, the Port would not have survived for over 800 years, if those who were responsibe for its development had relented to the pressure of sceptics. The Commercial Docks have, by virtue of their throughput, provided substantial support for the local economy. It is therefore essential that any future changes continue to promote the position of the Port and ensure that, together with the Town, it will uphold the name of - GREAT Grimsby.

The timber terraces that once occupied the South Side of the West Arm now form part of the car storage area alongside Alexandra Dock. As commercial traffic declined during the 1960's and 1970's, the water space became an ideal location for the pursuit of educational and leisure activities. These have now had to be curtailed owing to the increased movements of shipping. The Grimsby & Cleethorpes Yacht Club however, has retained its moorings adjacent to the A180 road bridge over Alexandra Dock. The majority of yachts have been removed from the water and can be seen on the land just to the east of the entrance to the Old Dock. (Geoff Byman)

It is always worth remembering that:-
THE EVENTS OF TODAY FORM THE HISTORY OF TOMORROW

The Gallery

A collection of bygone images featuring some of the people, locations and landmark events that have helped to shape the Port's long and distinguished history.

Cyclists wait behind the chain whilst Corporation Bridge is opened for shipping. Unlike the present structure the old bridge employed a swinging action thereby allowing vessels to pass between two wooden piers. (ABP)

Time to relax for a group of BTDB staff as they arrive at Skegness in 1967.

Onlookers gather to greet the Queen and the Duke of Edinburgh as they make their way towards the 70ft lock after disembarking from their launch at the Royal Dock Basin during their visit to the Port on 28 June 1958. (Grimsby Evening Telegraph)

The Port Master Grimsby & Immingham, James Lacey and his wife (seated centre) are joined by staff at a social event held at the Royal Hotel during the early 1960's. The photograph also includes Harry Burnicle (Assistant Port Master), Mike Clarke, John Craven, Captain Richard Freeman (Dock Master, Grimsby), Gladys Hoult (Port Master's Secretary), Arthur Hull (later to become Assistant Docks Manager), Gordon Kendall, Brian Lingard, Christine Milner, Clive Simpson and Alan Shucksmith. (ABP)

Don Popplewell, the last of the dock pilots to take vessels from the locks to their berths on arrival and vice versa upon departure is seen resting on 'his' bollard. In order for him to provide an additional securing point for vessels berthing at the Nor-Cargo Terminal he asked whether an additional bollard could be installed. In meeting his request the Port Authority duly obliged. Prior to becoming a boatman and dock pilot he served as a deck officer on the 'Flatiron Colliers' which carried coal from the ports of North East England, including Grimsby, to the power stations on the Thames. (Chris Turner)

The Dock Police were associated with the Port for many years, originally occupying accommodation within the Dock Offices. This group, photographed in 1895 outside the main entrance, includes a number of Officers proudly wearing medals gained during the Crimean War. (Great Central Society).

A group of coal trimmers take a break on the Coaling Jetty. (NELC Welholme Galleries)

Deck apprentices from the Nautical Department of Grimsby College taking part in the 1962 Regatta held in Alexandra Dock. This annual event was organised by Mr. Frank Priest, Divisional Officer of the Department. (Frank Priest Jnr.)

The Port Master, Captain F. Mortimer Barwick, surrounded by his staff on the steps of the Dock Offices in June 1918. (ABP)

A group of Sea Scouts on board H.M.S. M.T.B. 770 named the 'Rolls Royce' berthed on the West Side of the South Arm, Alexandra Dock in 1949. These were just a few of the many boys trained at facilities based in Alexandra Dock over the years before entering the Royal Navy, Merchant Navy or joining Grimsby's fishing fleet. (Grimsby Evening Telegraph)

Corporation Bridge with the clock tower at Central Market in the background. Given to the Town by Edward Bannister during his term in office as Mayor, the clock tower stood 40 feet (12.19 metres) in height and had two faces located 20 feet (6.10 metres) above the ground. It was demolished in 1959 when the clock was removed and taken to Cadwell Park motor racing circuit. (ABP)

Corporation Bridge looking towards Corporation Road with the tram station on the right of the photograph. The bridge was opened in 1873 and remained in operation until 1926. It was replaced in 1928 by the present structure. (ABP)

A solitary policeman stands on Corporation Bridge taking account of shipping movements in Alexandra Dock. The bridge eventually started to experience mechanical problems. In February 1921 the winch stripped a number of cogs resulting in the need to hire a tug at a cost of £2/10s (£2-50p) per day in order to pull the bridge open. (ABP)

The new Corporation Bridge under construction in 1928. It was opened by Edward, Prince of Wales on 19 July of the same year. (ABP)

Barges berthed at the rear of Victoria Mill. This building has formed part of the Town's skyline for many years. It was erected in 1906 and originally occupied by William Marshall. In later years it was taken over by Spillers who remained in the premises until the early 1960's when they decided to relocate their flour processing business to Gainsborough. The property gradually started to decline although Nickerson Seeds had an interest in the building until the 1980's when they eventually vacated. It now forms a pleasant apartment complex with views over the Dock for those living at the rear. (ABP)

The River Head in the 1960's with Sowerby's Mill to the left of the photograph. On the opposite side was South Dock Street with its old commercial buildings accomodating businesses including N. Blow & Company (Wharfingers), M. Kitching & Company (Cattle Foods) and Furness (Builders Merchants) Limited. On the corner of River Head and Victoria Street many may remember Cussins the furniture store with its large plate glass windows and modern appearance. (Garry Crossland)

Looking along West Dock Street towards Flottergate, with the Haven Mill to the right in the background. It is not difficult to see that the road follows the present alignment of Fredrick Ward Way, which was created along the North Side of the former Baxtergate car park. During the 1960's it was proposed that the adjoining Haven be culverted and infilled to increase the number of car parking spaces in the Town. (Garry Crossland)

The M.V. 'Delta' berthed in the West Arm, Alexandra Dock. The two embankments that served the Coaling Jetty, constructed in the mid 1870's, can just be seen, to the left, in the background. (NELC Local Studies Library.)

Above 'Fairtry III' was one of a fleet of vessels that visited the Port to discharge their cargoes of whale meat during the 1950's. Over a period of time they visited both Grimsby and Immingham and were often crewed by personnel recruited from the area. The cold store in the background, originally constructed by the Great Northern Railway, as a warehouse, was ideally located to receive cargoes from the 'Fairtry III' and her sister vessels. (ABP)

Left The M.V. 'Northland' moored in the centre of the Royal Dock discharging a cargoe of halibut. She was a mother ship designed to store the catches from a fleet of twelve accompanying steam trawlers specially adapted for line fishing. Her flotilla of eight motorised boats ferried the fish from the liners and loaded it into her hold where it remained until she returned to Port. During her voyage to Greenland in 1932 it was proposed that the group aim to catch 2,500 tons of halibut. In order to achieve this a total of 445 men were involved, 200 of which were based on the 'Northland'. They commenced work 500 miles to the north of Cape Farewell but after encountering bad weather and experiencing various other problems the venture became a failure. When the season ended a Norwegian whaling company purchased the 'Northland'. (David Cowell)

Left Stevedores man-handle bagged cargo on the East Side, Royal Dock. (NELC Welholme Gallaries.)

Below Business and pleasure combine as these two vessels follow a course to their separate berths in Alexandra Dock. The 'Hetaera', skippered by the late and sadly missed Gerry Hanniford is bound for the Grimsby & Cleethorpes Yacht Club. (Chris Turner)

Above Discharging frozen strawberries for Ross Foods.

Right A general view of shipping in the Royal Dock including the former fisheries research vessel the 'Ernest Holt'. (ABP)

The last visit of the successor to the 'Ernest Holt', the 'Cirolana', berthed on the East Side, Royal Dock. (ABP)

Looking towards the Dock Offices, the accumulator tower on the West Side of the 70ft lock provides an ideal vantage point to survey the Royal Dock. A complement of cranes on both sides of the Dock together with the sheer legs, to the right of the photograph, and the coaling appliances on the central jetty offer comprehensive facilities for the handling of a wide range of cargoes. (NELC Local Studies Library)

A small fleet of Naval vessels berth alongside Wintringham & Son Limited, one of the many timber companies located adjacent to Alexandra Dock. The houses in the background formed part of the West Marsh area of the Town and the chimney to the left of centre marks Peter Dixon's paper mill. (Grimsby Evening Telegraph)

Demolishing the Dock Master's House on the West side of the lock. The Railway Company provided this accommodation when the Royal Dock was constructed in order to enable its senior marine employee to live adjacent to his main place of work. (ABP)

The herring slip was often the scene of intense activity particularly when the visiting herring luggers had been following the shoals of fish down the East Coast. This structure, together with the West Pier, was originally constructed to form a tidal basin outside the entrance to the Royal Dock. It was used as a harbour to accommodate the first fleets of fishing vessels before No. 1 Fish Dock was opened in 1856. (NELC Welholme Galleries)

The statue of Prince Albert was originally located in the gardens opposite the Royal Hotel. However following the decision to construct the Cleethorpe Road flyover, which was opened in October 1968, it was repositioned outside the Dock Offices. (ABP)

This aerial view of the Royal Dock clearly shows the former railway station and the Dock Master's House, both of which have now been demolished. The sheer legs (arrowed) that can also be seen on the West Side of the Dock have also been removed. Sheer legs were used for lifting heavy machinery that could not be handled by the traditional quayside cranes. Pivoted at its base, the top of the 'A' frame could be raised or lowered in order to manoeuvre its load into or out of vessels berthed at the adjacent quay. Unfortunately after being damaged by a DFDS vessel it was decided that the sheer legs should be abandoned, resulting in their eventual demolition in December 1974. (NELC Local Studies Library)

The shed accommodation that covered the herring slip was demolished in 1952. Here we can see the first stages being removed. (Grimsby Evening Telegraph)

Top and Bottom   An extraordinary accident occurred on Tuesday 12 September 1911. A chain hanging from a quayside crane on the West Side of the Royal Dock caught in a rail wagon as it was being shunted along the track. Frank Doughty, a crane lad, witnessed the incident and mounted the crane in order to let out the chain. At the same time other workers tried to stop the engine driver but to no avail. Eventually when the whole length of the chain had been let out the crane toppled over onto the quay. Miraculously Doughty escaped serious injury and only suffered from cuts and severe shaking. (NELC Local Studies Library)

Salvage work underway to recover the bucket dredger 'Foremost Glen' in the Royal Dock Basin on 6 April 1962. (ABP)

One of the most serious fires of the time occurred on Saturday 22 November 1913. Four acres of timber on the North Side of Alexandra Dock was destroyed as flames engulfed the premises of Messrs. Joseph Green and Company. Both the Borough and Dock Fire Brigades attended the blaze but they were unable to reduce the intensity of the heat sufficiently to stop the rail tracks from being buckled and twisted. The total damage caused was estimated to be between £30,000 and £60,000. (NELC Local Studies Library)

The funnel of the tug 'Lady Cecilia' can be seen just above the water between the Coaling Jetty and No. 7 Berth. The tug had originally been moored alongside the jetty, but when the water in the dock started to rise the insufficient slack in her mooring ropes caused the vessel to develop a list. Water flooded through an open hatch thereby resulting in her journey to the bottom of the dock. circa 1959 (ABP)

The M.V. 'Giannis' seen here in November 1963 appears to have experienced an extremely rough passage. It was not, however, uncommon for timber vessels to develop a list if their cargoes shifted in bad weather. It was important to ensure that when they eventually entered Port they were discharged as quickly and cautiously as possible. It would not be in the interest of the Port Authority or the vessel owners for the ship to roll over and rest on the bottom of the dock. (ABP)

Bibliography

Anderson P. (1992) Railways of Lincolnshire (Irwell Press)

Associated British Ports (1994/95) Grimsby & Immingham Port Handbook

British Transport Docks Board and DFDS (1964 - 1967) Correspondence and Reports

British Transport Docks Board (5th November 1964) Letter: Hydraulic Tower, Royal Dock

British Transport Docks Board (May 1968) Handbook to accompany the visit of the Board to Grimsby & Immingham Docks

British Transport Docks Board (March 1971) The Port of Grimsby & Immingham

British transport Docks Board (1977/78) Grimsby & Immingham Docks Handbook

Clark E.D. (1864) Description of the Great Grimsby (Royal) Dock (The Institution of Civil Engineers)

DFDS (1991) Ship Development Through 125 Years

D'Orley A. A. (June 1968) The Humber Ferries (Nidd Valley Narrow Gauge Railways Limited)

Drinkell A. (1989) Shipbuilding and Repairing at Lock Hill Outfall

Drury E. The Great Grimsby Story (Drury)

Drury E. (1991) The Greater Grimsby Story (Drury)

Gerlis D. & L. (1986) The Grimsby Jewish Community (Humberside Leisure Services)

Gillett E. (1970) A History of Grimsby (University of Hull Press)

Great Central Railway Company (c.1911) Commercial Guide and Gazetteer

Great Central Railway (1911) The Port of Grimsby & Immingham

Great Central Railway (1st October 1912) Timetable: To and from The Continent via Grimsby

Great Central Railway (1913) Per Rail

Great Central Railway (20th April 1921) Report: G.C.R. Steamships. Outline of History

Grimsby As It Was (1974) D. Boswell and J. M. Storey (Hendon Publishing Company Limited)

Grimsby As It Was Vol. II (1976) D. Boswell and J. M. Storey (Hendon Publishing Company Limited)

Grimsby Borough of (1968) Official Guide (Faber Advertising)

Grimsby Evening Telegraph (14th October 1954) Victoria Street Centenary 1854 - 1954

Grimsby Evening Telegraph (4th February 1955) Article: Sun fruit comes to Grimsby

Grimsby Evening Telegraph (3rd January 1969)   Article: Hovercraft Arrives-Begins final trials on the Humber

Grimsby Evening Telegraph (27th January 1988) Article: Nor-Cargo 40th Anniversary

Grimsby Evening Telegraph (23rd May 1990) Article : Multi-Million Pound Grimsby Port Plan

Grimsby Telegraph (12th September 1911) Article: Extraordinary Accident on the Docks

Grimsby Telegraph (24th November 1913) Article: Huge Blaze at Grimsby

Grimsby Telegraph (10th September 1923) Article: Dock Tower Death

Grimsby Haven Act (1796)

Grimsby Haven Company (1805) Description of the New Wet Dock at Grimsby

Grimsby News (25th June 1897) Diamond Jubilee Supplement

Hurst T.J. Project Report: The River Freshney

Jackson Gordon (1971) Grimsby and the Haven Company (Grimsby Public Libraries)

Kay David (1981) The Book of Grimsby (Barracuda Books Limited)

King P.K. & Hewins D.R. (1988) The Railways Around Grimsby (Foxline Publishing)

Lincoln Bob (1913) The Rise of Grimsby Vol I (Farnol, Eades, Irvine and Company)

London and North Eastern Railway Company (1931) Ports of the LNER

London and North Eastern Railway Company (c.1944) Report: History of the Railway during the war - Docks

Modern Transport (16th December 1922) Humber Ports Issue

Newton Lee R. (27th & 28th February 1796) Correspondence with Mr. G. Babb

John Sutcliffe & Son (1987) A History of the Company 1862-1987

The Illustrated London News Article: Great Grimsby Dock